Will Campbell

Will Campbell:

Radical Prophet of the South

Merrill M. Hawkins, Jr.

Mercer University Press
Macon, Georgia

ISBN 0-86554-562-6   MUP/H422

Copyright ©1997
Mercer University Press, Macon, Georgia 31210-3960 USA
All rights reserved
Printed in the United States of America

Library of Congress Cataloging-in-Publication Data

Hawkins, Merrill M. Jr., 1963-
    Will Campbell: Radical Prophet of the South /Merrill M. Hawkins,
Jr.
        xi + 206 pp.   6" x 9" (15 x 22 cm.)
    Includes bibliographical references and index.
    ISBN 0-86554-562-6 (alk. paper)
1. Campbell, Will D. 2. Baptists—United States—Clergy—Biography.
3. Civil rights workers—United States—Biography. 4. Afro-Ameri-
cans—Civil rights—Southern States.   5.   Southern States—Race
Relations. I. Title.
BX6495.C28H38 1997
286'.1'092—dc21
[B]

To Kimberly and Anna Lee

Contents

Acknowledgments

The writing of this book represents the recent—and not so recent—work and influence of the many people to whom I owe great debts. This project started as my dissertation, and I offer my gratitude to the members of my committee, William L. Pitts, Glenn O. Hilburn, and Stanley W. Campbell. These professors influenced me during my classes, as well as during their guidance of the dissertation. Professor Hilburn provided much positive encouragement to me to complete the study. I offer a special thanks to Professor Campbell for his insightful conversations, extending back to my undergraduate years, on this and other related topics. I especially appreciate Professor Pitts who directed the dissertation and mentored me during the four years I worked as his graduate assistant.

I developed an interest in the history of Christianity while studying at Southwestern Baptist Theological Seminary under Leon McBeth, who introduced me to the discipline and encouraged me to pursue further studies. Bill Leonard, Dean of the School of Divinity at Wake Forest University, spoke with me by phone in preparation for my personal interview of Campbell. His suggestion that I explore Campbell's ecclesiology shaped the approach of Chapter Three. Jonathan Lindsey of Baylor University looked at my preliminary studies of Will Campbell and offered valuable suggestions about style and content. Glenn Jonas of Campbell University, a colleague from graduate school days, provided sound advice during all stages of this project. He made extra efforts to read my manuscript and offer suggestions, ever eager to discuss the topic in particular and and its relationship to American religious history. A collective thanks is extended to the staff of Moody Library. The holdings of the library contained almost all the sources I needed. Barbara Cantrell's work through interlibrary loan gathered the books and articles not in the Moody collection. Naomi Leavell of the University of Mississippi Archives was helpful in helping me secure information about the Ole Miss faculty in the 1950s.

I came to my present place of employment, the Department of Religion at Carson-Newman College after my dissertation was completed and my revisions were underway. My thanks goes to my colleagues in the department, as well as the administration, for supporting and encouraging this work. I owe a special thanks to Mark Seagroves of Carson-Newman for assisting me with the printing of one of the copies of the manuscript. The college was especially supportive by allowing me a work schedule that allowed time in the spring of 1997 to finish revisions. The editors and publishers at Mercer University Press have been a source of encouragement during the last two years of conversations. My gratitude goes particularly to Andrew Manis, Marc Jolley, and Vaughn CroweTipton for their interest in this work and their creative suggestions about style and presentation.

I am deeply grateful to the subject of this study, Will D. Campbell. When I decided to study an aspect of his work, I called Campbell to determine his feelings about the matter. He has been a tremendous personal resource, taking time to speak with me over the phone. Campbell's willingness to grant me an extensive interview in December 1992 at his home in Nashville and to give me two phone interviews made this dissertation possible. My admiration for the man as a social activist and writer was great when I started this study. My admiration for him as a person as I complete the study is even greater.

A number of relatives have shared the experience of this study. My parents, Merrill and Carrie Hawkins, have shown an interest in this work and offered their fine skills as proofreaders. This was not the first time they have heard me talk at length about a subject that commands all my attention. My father was also diligent in reminding me of my editor's deadline in most every conversation we had the first half of 1997. My in-laws, Douglas and Joyce Tanner, have also given encouragement during all phases of this work.

Finally, I want to thank my wife, Kimberly, for her unconditional support during all aspects of my graduate education. Kim read my manuscript and helped conduct my interview with Campbell. She has shared my interest in Campbell, and our conversations helped me form my thought about this project. I value her professional opinion, and I appreciate her assistance with this project. During the early stages of this project, Kimberly worked as a school teacher, and she was always willing to help in any manner with this work, even in the middle of her very busy days. During the final stages of writing and research, we shared the birth of our first child, Anna Lee. That made her days no less busy, yet it did not dimimish her interest in the project. It is to them I give thanks and for them I am thankful.

Merrill M. Hawkins, Jr.
Jefferson City, Tennessee

Chapter 1

A Baptist from the South:
A Biographical Sketch

In 1977 Will D. Campbell published *Brother to a Dragonfly*, an autobiography highlighting his relationship with his troubled brother and his experiences as a civil rights activist in the American South.[1] Perhaps his best-known book, *Brother to a Dragonfly* launched Campbell in a new direction as a writer. In the years since this book's publication, Campbell published seven books, five fictional and two autobiographical, all of which critique institutional religion and offer his vision of authentic religion. For Campbell, the institutional church and authentic Christianity, while not always antithetical, are not synonymous. *Brother to a Dragonfly*, *Forty Acres and a Goat*, and *Providence* all describe Campbell's eventual disillusionment with conventional and non-conventional religious groups. In describing his own self-awareness, Campbell said:

> I resolved to be a Baptist preacher of the South until the day I die. Though never again a Southern Baptist preacher. For the first time, I knew there was a difference. And what it was.[2]

Since 1963 Campbell has worked out of his home in Tennessee. For a time, the Committee of Southern Churchmen, funded by several organizations such as the Southern Regional Council, paid him a small salary.[3] Since the 1970s Campbell's primary income has come from his work as an author. In addition to

---

[1]Campbell, *Brother to a Dragonfly* (New York: Continuum, 1977).
[2]Campbell, *Forty Acres and a Goat: A Memoir* (Atlanta: Peachtree, 1986), 146.
[3]*Forty Acres and a Goat*, 86.

writing books, Campbell has written extensively for a variety of periodicals, especially *Christianity and Crisis*. He has worked to apply his concern for African Americans to all dispossessed peoples. Consequently, Campbell has been an advocate for a number of humanitarian causes, including prison reform and support for poor whites. Although still a social activist, Campbell has become a voice for religiously-oriented activists dissatisfied with utopian solutions to social problems.

Campbell has expressed his view of religion, society, and human nature in the tradition of Christian radicalism.[4] Rejecting conventional approaches to religion, his views are now expressed in a variety of motifs, including Anabaptist and Baptist models and the idea of religion as a constitutive element in Southern culture. Though informed by neo-orthodoxy, Campbell hesitates to admit any rigid theological categories in his thought. He does, however, acknowledge that the Christian anarchy of Jacques Ellul and Vernard Eller resemble his thought. This book examines Campbell's social and religious thought, and emphasizes the sources that influenced his religious development and the various means by which Campbell has expressed his views.

Undergirding the various models used by Campbell is a mistrust of all institutional structures, a mistrust acquired from his personal experience and expressed in neo-orthodox terminology. Thus, the first chapter discusses the events that led Campbell in that direction. After Campbell developed his mature world view and left the institutional church, he continued to address social issues. He did not address these issues from a secular point of view, however. He spoke out on issues, freely using faith-informed language. The second chapter addresses the issues that continued to be of importance to Campbell after leaving the National Council. Finally, while Campbell has expressed himself through a variety of modes since 1963, two in particular are representative and will be the subject of the final chapters: the theme of

---

[4]Biographical information drawn from Samuel S. Hill, Jr., ed. *Encyclopedia of Religion in the South* (Macon: Mercer University Press, 1984), 180-181.

Baptist/Anabaptist ecclesiology and the method of autobiography. These two modes express his mature social and religious thought because they reflect individualism, a religious world view, and an affirmation of his place within the southern culture of the United States.

Preparation for Conventional Ministry

Will Davis Campbell always thought of himself as a preacher. When he was a young boy growing up in south Mississippi, he felt destiny and family influence thrust him into the world of religious vocation. Of all the Campbell children, Will Davis was "the one marked to be the preacher."[5] When he worked for the NCC's Department of Racial and Cultural Relations, Campbell continued to think of himself as a preacher, not a "social engineer."[6] Even after his departure from the National Council of Churches, which marked the end of any traditional ministry, he still thought of himself as a preacher. At this point in the development of his thought, Campbell separated the work of a preacher from employment in the structures of institutional religion.[7]

In each of these periods in his life, he consistently understood his role as motivated by religion, specifically Christianity. When he made a transition from one role to another, he did so not simply out of disillusionment, but out of an effort to live in accord with his own religious values. Whether pursuing an education, serving as a traditional minister, working as a social activist, or withdrawing to his farm in Mount Juliet, Tennessee, Will Campbell operated out of his sense of religious truth.

As he evolved from traditional minister to civil rights activist, Campbell grew disillusioned with convention ministry and social activism, eventually reassessing his own "calling." As he exited traditional forms of ministry and activism, Campbell had been

---

[5]*Brother to a Dragonfly*, 43.
[6]Second interview by author.
[7]*Forty Acres and a Goat*, 147-148.

molded into a religiously-oriented, anti-institutional activist. These perspectives have governed his thought and actions since 1963, when he left the NCC.

Born in Amite County, Mississippi in 1924, Will Campbell was the fifth generation of Campbells to live in the southwestern corner of this southern state. Campbell's paternal great-great-grandfather moved from Georgia to the region while Mississippi was still a territory.[8] By the time of Will's birth in 1924, the family's roots were well-established in the rural community of East Fork. His father, Lee Webb, was a farmer, while his mother was a traditional housewife.[9] Campbell was the third child born to this home, with an older sister and brother, Lorraine and Joe.[10] A fourth child, Paul Edward, completed the family.

Like all families, the Campbells had their share of problems and their measure of happiness. Campbell's mother often awoke at night with terrible stomach pains, originally diagnosed as ulcers. The cries of pain awoke the entire family and set a nightly ritual in motion. Campbell's father first tried to console the mother and convince her that she was not dying, which always failed. Eventually, Joe was sent to contact the family physician, who lied twenty miles away. The doctor's brief examinations always resulted in the same prescription, which eased the pain and helped the patient fall asleep, although it would often be morning by the time relief came. In reality, however, Campbell's mother suffered from hypochondria.[11] In addition to her hypochondria, Campbell's mother was

---

[8]"An Oral History with Will Davis Campbell, Christian Preacher," interview by Orley B. Caudill, in *The Mississippi Oral History Program of the University of Southern Mississippi*, vol. 157 (Hattiesburg: University of Southern Mississippi, 1980), 2-3.

[9]*Brother to a Dragonfly*, 28.

[10]His older brother, subject of *Brother to a Dragonfly*, was Joe. Campbell, interview by Robert Dibble, in "An Investigative Study of Faith Development in the Adult Life and Works of Will D. Campbell" (Ed.D. diss., New Orleans Baptist Theological Seminary, 1984), 145-146.

[11]*Brother to a Dragonfly*, 54.

prone to emotional outbursts. After frequent quarrels with her husband, she would flee to the woods, only returning after an extensive search by her oldest son, Joe.

Campbell's father had problems of his own, but they were problems common to that era. Although Lee Webb Campbell owned an eighty-acre farm, agriculture—at least on small farms—had been robbed of its economic viability by the Great Depression. Lee Campbell accepted employment with the Works Progress Administration. Unable to make the transition from the autonomy of an agrarian lifestyle to a more structured routine, the elder Campbell lost his job.[12] This transition required the family to supplement its farm income with government assistance. Soon, Campbell's father was diagnosed with a heart murmur and was unable to work at all. His sons, Will and Joe, took over the work of the farm. The older brother, Joe, served as manager.[13] Adulthood came early for the children.

Campbell's childhood was not all drudgery. In spite of the hardship, or perhaps because of it, the children formed especially close bonds. Lorraine served a maternal role for the boys, while Joe, two years older than Will, served a paternal role. Although they often engaged in childhood fighting, the "four Campbell children—Lorraine, Joseph Lee, Will Davis, Paul Edward were a community."[14] The mature Campbell never recalled having a sense of hardship during his childhood and youth. He believed that his childhood blended the good and the bad, but he did not have strong memories of an unhappy childhood. Although Campbell grew up economically deprived, the entire community was deprived, so he did not sense deprivation. "Life was generally hard work," Campbell recalled, but he did not "recall words like 'happy' or 'boredom,' ever being a part of our vocabulary. . . ." Campbell

---

[12]Ibid., 28, 55.
[13]Ibid., 11, 40-41.
[14]Ibid., 41.

remembered "happiness" and "unhappiness." However, the feelings were not "known by those terms."[15]

Campbell's family was active in the only white church in his community, East Fork Baptist Church, where his father was a deacon.[16] Lee Campbell had considered becoming a minister as a young boy, but his lack of formal education later discouraged him from pursuing that goal. As a reminder of his childhood ambition, the father's nickname became "Preacher," a term that remained with him as an adult.[17]

When he was only seven, Will decided that he wanted to become a member of the church. Because Baptists did not practice infant baptism or have a formal catechism, people joined the church only when they could declare a personal desire to do so. Several factors, however, drew Will to join the church at an earlier age than was typical. One Sunday young Will attended a church service that was interrupted by a local resident whose house was on fire. When the man came to the church for help, "'[i]t was at the very time the preacher was telling of the horrors of eternity in a burning hell." At the end of this same service, Campbell's brother joined the church. The traumatic sermon on hell and its unintentional illustration with the burning home, combined with the fortuitous example of his older brother, provided mixed influences drawing Campbell to church membership.

A short time later, Campbell asked his brother to advise him on becoming a member of the church. Although his brother initially discouraged him because of his youth, Campbell persisted in his interest. His brother told him that at the close of the service the minister would exhort people "to go down the aisle during the invitation hymn." If a person who had never publicly embraced the Baptist faith came forward during this hymn, that person was "a candidate for baptism if the vote [of the congregation] was

---

[15]Caudill interview, 3.
[16]Dibble interview, 145.
[17]*Brother to a Dragonfly*, 43.

favorable." Campbell later narrated what he interpreted as his first conversion:

> On the appointed night Joe sat beside me on the third bench from the front. He said if we were further back, where boys our age generally sat, it would be harder to do. On the first word of the invitational hymn Joe nudged me and I moved quietly and quickly past him and down the aisle. With Joe as catechist I had no trouble fielding the questions. Yes, I repented of all my sins, intended to lead a new life, and desired to follow Jesus in baptism.[18]

By joining the church at this early age, Campbell formally identified with the religious ethos of his community and his family. Campbell saw religion as a pervasive influence on his entire social environment, whether it was family, school, or personal relationships. "Religion simply flowed into school and school into family, and all of the social institutions . . . were not nearly as sharply divided [as today]."

The religious influence of his family reflected the community values. The white community was overwhelmingly Southern Baptist. In the local school, all the children, except for those of one family, belonged to the Baptist Church. Campbell did not recall "any Methodists, Presbyterians, certainly Episcopalians, Catholics or Jews" in the area.[19] Not only did religion have a pervasive influence, it was a particular type of religion. To be religious in the East Fork community was to be Baptist. Diversity and pluralism were not yet factors in rural Mississippi.

The religious environment of Campbell's family also drew him into an interest in the ministry at an early age. When the Camp-

---

[18]Ibid., 36-37. Campbell used the idea of conversion to describe major transitions and flashes of insight. He calls his reading of Howard Fast's *Freedom Road* his second conversion, and his response to the murder of civil rights worker Jonathan Daniels his third conversion. The religious nature of these later conversions, however, grows out of this childhood experience.

[19]Caudill interview, 4.

bell family argued, Campbell's emotional mother often told him that God would take his life as a punishment to the others. His early death, she prophesied, would serve as a catalyst to reunite the family, "who would thereafter live in peace and harmony." In looking back on the incidents, Campbell believed that this type of pressure initially motivated him to enter the ministry.

When he was five years old, Campbell became ill with pneumonia, which in that era without antibiotics, was often fatal. When Will failed to improve, he was diagnosed with pneumonia in both lungs, and the family feared that he would die. As a last resort, the family hired a nurse to give continual care and the boy recovered.[20]

Campbell's parents, however, did not believe that the nurse's efforts alone restored his health. They made a vow that if Campbell recovered, they would see that he became a minister. After his recovery, he was aware of the vow and "lived with that." As a result, from this early age Campbell was drawn to a ministerial career. In assessing the influences that drew him to religious work, he said, "I was always going to be a preacher." Campbell did not necessarily reject these experiences in his later life, calling them "as good a way to receive a divine call as any; as a burning bush or anything else."[21]

The community quickly began to think of Will as a budding young preacher. In local revival meetings, he was frequently called on to say public prayers. The audiences became impressed with his "long and well-worded prayers," and word spread that he "sounded for the world like a preacher praying." Campbell's childhood pastor, J. Price Brock, soon took an interest in cultivating Will's potential as a minister. The young Campbell began traveling with his pastor to various churches on the circuit, where Campbell observed his new mentor. Brock also encouraged Campbell to read. The books were not necessarily theological works. Brock wanted his protégée to read one book that dealt with overcoming timidity. The incident was perhaps the first time that Campbell realized that

---

[20]Ibid., 42, 43-45.
[21]Dibble interview, 8.

"practical and social habits as that seemed more important than what I might believe about one theological point or another. . . . The training was for success, not for faithfulness to Christian orthodoxy."

After this preliminary exposure to the ministry, the time arrived for Campbell to deliver his first sermon. A youth-led service at the church served as the occasion for his debut. For several weeks Campbell practiced his sermon, which was based on the creation account of Genesis. Although Campbell described himself as a "sixteen-year-old fundamentalist," the sermon reminded the audience that "the Bible had to do with earth and what happened there and not with heaven. . . . For some reason which I have never understood I had never taken much to preachments about other worlds—above or below."

Nonetheless, his premiere as a minister was an epiphany, both for himself and for the friends and family in attendance. Despite the worldly tone of the sermon, Campbell still focused on traditional moralisms, criticizing the congregation "for being irregular at Sunday night services," a criticism the audience enjoyed. So supportive were those in attendance, however, that Campbell said

> I could have denounced Christianity as a capitalistic myth cunningly designed to keep the masses under control, and our youth choir could have sung Ukrainian folk songs, and our Sunday School superintendent could have lectured on "The Origin of Species," and all the people would have said "Amen."[22]

Before he left for college, the same church ordained Campbell. Southern Baptist polity and practice make ordination a function of a local congregation. There are no specific requirements, such as education or a minimum age. The sole criterion is that the person seeking ordination be approved by a church-appointed council. After a council approves a candidate, the local congregation sets

---

[22]Ibid., 75-78.

the person apart in a fairly typical ordination service. A council composed of his father, his uncle, his cousin, and the minister examined his theology. Most of the questions were simple, although the minister asked him about the virgin birth and the verbal inspiration of the scriptures, doctrines that he "had never heard . . . discussed at all."[23] He gave satisfactory answers and one week later the council "would join with the others of the faithful of the East Fork Baptist Church in a ritual setting me apart to the Gospel ministry."[24]

Education and Professional Training

Ordained during his senior year in high school, Campbell was encouraged to train for the ministry. Over the next several years, Campbell attended a Baptist school at Pineville, Louisiana. Louisiana College was not the typical route for ministerial students from south Mississippi. The typical young man who wanted to be a Baptist minister and desired formal education followed a set pattern. First, one went to Southwest Junior College in nearby Summit. After two years there, Mississippi College in Clinton was the next step, followed by professional training at New Orleans Baptist Theological Seminary. As late as the summer after his high school graduation, Campbell still planned to take the first conventional step by enrolling at Southwest.[25]

That summer, however, Campbell preached at the Southside Baptist Church in nearby McComb.[26] In the audience was Tom Sharp, native to the area and by that time an executive for the Standard Oil Company in Baton Rouge. Sharp was impressed with the zeal of the young preacher and wanted to aid his ministerial training. For some unknown reason, Sharp wanted the young Campbell to bypass the traditional path of education and attend

---

[23]Caudill interview, 6.
[24]*Brother to a Dragonfly*, 129.
[25]Second interview by author.
[26]Caudill interview, 9.

Louisiana College. Campbell, however, was too shy to discuss the matter; hence, Sharp traveled to the Campbell residence to discuss it with his father. After visiting with Campbell's father, Sharp and Will rode to Pineville the following weekend, and Will registered immediately. Until that weekend he had never heard of Louisiana College, often confusing it with the larger public institution, Louisiana State University.[27]

Although Baptists established scattered congregations early in Louisiana, they had a difficult time establishing them in major cities. This difficulty naturally extended to Baptist efforts to establish a state denominational organization. Three attempts were made at starting a Baptist church in New Orleans; all failed. Only on the fourth attempt, in 1843, did the congregation eventually known as First Baptist become established. Baton Rouge did not have a permanent Baptist congregation until 1874.[28]

During the 1890s, Baptists succeeded in forming a unified state convention, consolidating several regional associations and drawing the New Orleans congregations into participation. In 1898 this expanded, more unified convention passed a resolution calling for an institution of higher education. Eight years later the first students arrived in Pineville to attend Louisiana College.[29]

Campbell arrived on campus for classes in 1941. The atmosphere at Louisiana College in the 1940s foreshadowed the coming World War. According to Campbell, the campus, was surrounded by machine guns and uniformed soldiers were on constant patrol, all part of a large war game exercise.[30] In spite of the military

---

[27]Ibid. After registering him at the college, Sharp brought Campbell back to his home to meet Mrs. Sharp. That same evening, the Sharps hosted a lecture in their home advocating Dispensationalism and Anglo-Israel theories, evidently to gain Campbell's interest in these ideas. Sharp and Campbell continued their relationship for about one year, after which it ended quietly. See *Brother to a Dragonfly*, 82-84.

[28]Samuel Hill, ed., *Encyclopedia of Religion in the South* (Macon, Georgia: Mercer University Press, 1984), s.v. "Louisiana," by Penrose St. Amant.

[29]Ibid.

[30]*Brother to a Dragonfly*, 85.

presence, Campbell settled in for what come to consider his most positive educational experience.

Campbell was not an outstanding student, by his own estimation. Much of his deficiency stemmed from weaknesses he had when he enrolled in college. "I could barely read and write when I went there," he mentioned in an interview. Of course, that self-assessment greatly underplayed his education. As a rather unathletic youth, Campbell typically avoided playing games with his friends. To compensate for his lack of skill he opted to read cowboy stories and write his own. He also wrote voluminously in grade school, often giving the teacher much more than the assigned minimum on essays.[31] While he certainly had deficiencies, he also displayed enough creativity to suggest the ability to pursue higher education.

Perhaps his limited horizons made him feel less than adequately prepared for college life. Before leaving for Pineville, Campbell had traveled no further from home than the ninety miles to New Orleans, and this trip he had made only once.[32] Campbell made the adjustment to college well, however. He met the woman he would later marry, and settled into all the activities of college life. In addition to taking classes, he worked with the campus newspaper and served as student pastor of a small country congregation, the Dodson Baptist Church, some fifty miles north of the campus.[33] In addition to these jobs, he worked part-time at a men's clothing store.[34]

Study naturally occupied some of Campbell's time, as well. Originally interested in philosophy, Campbell soon changed his major to English.[35] One of his English teachers, Hazel Hall, first taught him to diagram sentences. He also studied literature under William P. Carson, civics under W. Strouther, and Bible under J.

---

[31]Second interview by author.
[32]Dibble interview, 150.
[33]Second interview by author.
[34]*Brother to a Dragonfly*, 88.
[35]Second interview by author.

E. Brakefield. Actual study received low priority from Campbell.[36] Perhaps the growing sense that war was coming, as well as his own sense of inadequacy, caused his lack of attention. Academically, Campbell looked back on the credits he earned as "one and a half years of credits that were academically no good."[37] But the time was not ill-spent, and Campbell grew in other ways that he felt were as important as course grades. "Of all the schools I had attended," he recalled, "I learned more there than I had anywhere else." His statement that he "had more to learn" there than he did at the other schools implies that his college years involved the development of maturity as much as academic growth.[38]

His time at the small Baptist college positively influenced his value-system. "I learned a lot of things that don't go on transcripts at Louisiana College, a lot of things, a lot of values."[39] For the first time, he questioned the strong emphasis fundamentalist religion placed on moralisms as the essential element of the Christian faith.

> [T]he Christian faith . . . was pretty much a negative thing: don't smoke, don't drink liquor, don't mess around on Saturday night. And I rebelled pretty early against those things, pretty early in my theological development, even probably going back to Louisiana College.[40]

Essentially, Louisiana College was a place for Campbell to pass from adolescence into adulthood while living in an atmosphere that resembled family. Surprisingly, he credited the school's ability to provide that type of environment with its "small, religiously oriented" nature.[41] Permanent friendships formed during these

---

[36]*Brother to a Dragonfly*, 86; Oscar Hoffmeyer, *Louisiana College 75 Years: A Pictorial History* (Pineville, Louisiana: Louisiana College, 1981), 146-51.

[37]Caudill interview, 25.

[38]Second interview by author.

[39]Caudill interview, 25.

[40]Dibble interview, 151.

[41]Ibid.

years, as Campbell has kept in contact with more of these class-mates, than those from any other school he attended.[42]

Campbell did not graduate from Louisiana College. Even though he was ordained and eligible to opt out of military service, Campbell decided to waive his deferral. Many reasons influenced his decision, although the main reason was that his brother had already been drafted into the service.[43] In addition his failing grades and his lack of enthusiasm with the academic regimen led him consider dropping out. Because of his ministerial status, his local draft board refused to draft him. He tried to enlist, but his small stature met with rejection from the Army, Navy, and Marine Corps. Finally, the draft board reluctantly honored his petition to be removed from his exempt status. A short time later, he was drafted into the army.

Campbell did not see combat while stationed in the South Pacific, although his initial basic training was as a rifleman. Upon his arrival in New Caledonia, the Master Sergeant making assignments discovered that Campbell's uncle was a friend. That discovery prompted the Sergeant to pull Campbell's file, which informed him of the new recruit's declined ministerial deferral. Wanting to do a favor for Campbell's uncle, the sergeant intended to dismiss Campbell from service. While Campbell's strong protest kept him in active duty, it did not take him to the front. The sergeant saw that Campbell was assigned as an orderly in a safe army hospital.[44]

In many ways Campbell's military service was as important as his formal education. The years in the army allowed him more time to mature. Much of his maturity came not as much from the army experience itself as from his still being in a formative period of his life. There was, however, a certain amount of growth that resulted directly from the military experience. For the first time, Campbell came in close contact with people from different cultures

---

[42] Second interview by author.
[43] Ibid.
[44] *Brother to a Dragonfly*, 90-92.

and world views, including Jews, Cajuns, and Marxists.[45] This initial exposure to diversity increased his sensitivity to America's heterogeneity.[46]

More significantly, Campbell established a close relationship with his chaplain during these years. Stephen Crary, a graduate of Union Theological Seminary, spent many hours talking with Will about the implications of religious faith, including its impact on race. According to Campbell, Crary advocated some ideas about race that were particularly provocative to a young Southerner.[47] Neo-Orthodox in his thinking, Crary was also the first minister Campbell met with a theological orientation other than that of southern pietism[48]

In addition to his exposure to cultural diversity, Campbell surprisingly found time to read extensively.[49] At first, Campbell read leisure writings, such as *The Saturday Evening Post*. A fellow soldier from New York encouraged him to read instead what Campbell viewed as the rather leftist magazines, *The Protestant* and *The New York PM*.[50]

While Campbell's brother, Joe, was recovering from some injuries, he wrote recommending Howard Fast's *Freedom Road*, a book he promised "[will] turn your head around" on race relations.[51] Set in the Reconstruction Era South, *Freedom Road* is a fictionalized account of the short-lived political power of former slaves, and their alliance with the poor whites. The goal of this alliance, led by Gideon Jackson in the story, was the acquisition of property rights and economic opportunity, which the former slaves did not have, and the poor whites had only tenuously. Fearing that such an alliance would weaken their power, the planter class

---

[45] Caudill interview, 12-13.
[46] Dibble interview, 153.
[47] Caudill interview, 14.
[48] Dibble interview, 153.
[49] Second interview by author.
[50] Caudill interview, 13.
[51] *Brother to a Dragonfly*, 96.

conspired to rob African Americans of their power and to destroy their alliance with the poor whites by fomenting racial fear.[52]

Fast not only told the drama of Reconstruction but also argued that racial division was a result of economic class division and that the racial divisions between poor whites and former slaves were designed to serve the interests of the upper classes. Fast also used the Reconstruction Era to assess American racial conditions in 1944 from a Marxist perspective.[53]

Prior to reading Fast's book, Campbell had never thought much about racial issues. He essentially accepted the status quo of the South. Reading this book marked a turning point, which he called a conversion because it revolutionized his thinking about race in America. Campbell began to view traditional racial mores as a structural problem imposed on average people for the benefit of the wealthy, an idea he retained into his mature thought. He also identified with the poor whites of *Freedom Road*, now understanding his own people to be dispossessed.

Campbell did not see his emerging views on race as resulting from an enlightened political view. Indeed, he has said that he was unaware of Fast's relationship with the Communist party, and that "there was nothing that would attract me to any kind of left-wing politics at the time." The book's effect was more religious, containing "the most powerful and compelling words I had read in my nineteen years." His response to racism was intimately involved in his continuing interest in the ministry. Prior to that book, he had a very traditional concept of the role of the minister. "Without question," after this awakening he said, "I knew during that period that [social activism] would be the direction that my ministry would take."

---

[52]Howard Fast, *Freedom Road* (New York: Duell, Sloan, and Pearce, 1944).

[53]Deborah A. Straub, ed., "Fast, Howard, 1914-," *Contemporary Authors: New Revision Series* (Detroit: Gail Research, 1988). Fast was for a time a member of the American Communist Party, and wrote several novels from a Marxist perspective, including *Freedom Road*.

[It was] a rather abrupt and robust change of interest and direction from a kid who was going to be the traditional preacher and have three revivals a year and move on up the ladder and wind up as pastor of the First Baptist Church of Sumrall, Mississippi or somewhere.[54]

In addition to his reading of *Freedom Road*, other events while Campbell served in the Army affected his perspective on race. Working in the operating room one day, he attended a young native Caledonian suffering from a ruptured spleen. The injury resulted from a beating the boy sustained from his white employer. The question occurred to Campbell,"[W]hy did he do that? It was because this guy was a 'gook.' And it dawned on me, somewhat vaguely at the time, that's what we do back home."[55]

With his new perspective on race, Campbell wanted to put his thought into action. His first act of defiance against standard racial mores came while riding the troop train back to his home to be discharged. Seeing two African-American soldiers, Campbell deliberately befriended them because of their color. The three of them shared a bunk together, and acted as if the classic divisions between the races did not exist. Boarding the train in California, the group had little resistance to their friendship as they crossed the West and entered Texas. On moving into East Texas and approaching Texarkana, however, they began to notice the segregated facilities at each station. The segregated attitudes of some of the other soldiers became apparent as well. Asking to join a card game, Campbell was rejected because the group did not want to play with a "nigger-lover." For the first time, Campbell saw that his racial view "is going to cost you something. . . . You've got to decide now whether you're going to be serious."[56]

---

[54]On Fast's influence on Campbell, see Caudill interview, 13, 22; Dibble interview, 154; *Brother to a Dragonfly*, 96-97.

[55]Dibble interview, 152-153.

[56]Caudill interview, 16.

Serious, however, was precisely what Campbell intended to be. His experience in the Army had not only exposed him to new cultures and to a glimpse of formal theological training but also had moved him beyond his cultural upbringing on the question of race. Campbell doubts that he would have taken the same route if he had accepted his ministerial deferral from military duty. He is not certain why the experience was so formative, though, since many of his peers from Amite County served in the Army and returned to the South without any change of view.[57]

More than most of his peers, Campbell was ripe for responding to the influences he encountered. He was a nineteen-year-old minister with almost two years of college education, poor grades notwithstanding. He spent his spare time in the service reading broadly, from Howard Fast to the *Protestant*. And he developed a relationship with a Union Seminary-trained chaplain with a neo-orthodox background.

Most young men at this age are impressionable. Campbell happened to be impressed by forces that steered him toward a deeper commitment to social activism. This commitment impressed him enough to make him willing to challenge the conventional racial attitudes of his native South, a willingness few young white men acquired. The people he encountered in the army were different from those encountered by his peers from his home community, and they made him a different person.

After his discharge from the service, Campbell did not return to Louisiana College, despite his pleasant pre-war experience there. Instead, he opted to attend Wake Forest College, then located in Wake Forest, North Carolina. It was his first formal educational experience outside the deep South. He spent the next several years breaking away from southern culture and the strict piety of his youth. His education provided a way to make the break.

Many factors drew Campbell to this school so far from his roots. His relatively poor grades at Louisiana College contributed to his decision. A group of army friends from North Carolina told

---

[57]Dibble interview, 153.

him about Wake Forest College, a school unknown to Campbell. These people encouraged him to come to North Carolina, where they could continue their friendship. Campbell also needed to "mak[e] a new beginning" after his experiences in the military, and relocation to a new school in a different area provided that opportunity.[58]

The distance between Wake Forest and Louisiana College involved more than miles. In Campbell's estimation, Louisiana College was a "traditional Baptist institution." Wake Forest College [now University] was founded by the Baptists of North Carolina in 1833. Campbell felt, however, that Wake was less shaped by its denominational identity. Although "[i]t was a Baptist college [it was] far removed from" the typical denominational college. He found Wake Forest to be "really just one more liberal arts college," a characteristic he liked.[59]

Although Campbell graduated from Wake Forest, the school did not leave the lasting impression on Campbell that Louisiana College had. While he remembered some people from those days, he formed no lasting relationships.[60] Nothing in Campbell's interviews or writings, however, indicates an unpleasant experience at Wake Forest.

The lack of permanent relationships or impressions most likely stems from his increased maturity. At Louisiana College Campbell was a seventeen-year-old leaving home for the first time. A college student at that age has diverse interests, including social relationships as well as academics. The Campbell who arrived at Wake

---

[58]Second interview by author. "Quite a number of fellows in my unit were from North Carolina . . . and said, 'Come up to North Carolina and we'll get together every weekend.' I mean when the war was over those friendships dissolved and everybody went back to their own communities and families and interests, but that's why I went to Wake Forest."; Caudill interview, 25.

[59]Caudill interview, 25; On the history of Wake Forest College, see Hill, *The Encyclopedia of Religion in the South*, s.v. "North Carolina," by John Woodward. Wake Forest moved to Winston-Salem in 1956 and achieved university status in 1966.

[60]Dibble interview, 150.

Forest was not a mere college freshman, but a man with almost two years of college education, three years of military duty, and the prospect of marriage. In fact in 1946 Campbell married Brenda Fisher, his sweetheart from his Louisiana College days. Perhaps maturity simply made him less impressionable. Maturity, however, did not encourage Campbell to improve his grades, which remained mediocre. His goal at this stage in life was not a broad college experience as much as completing his degree so that he could enroll in divinity school.

Having completed his undergraduate education, Campbell was now ready for professional training as a minister. At this stage in his education, Campbell did not want to attend a traditional denominational seminary, especially a Southern Baptist school. His decision was shaped more by his desire to receive a prominent degree than by his theology. He was accepted at Union Theological Seminary in New York, but he was denied admission to Yale Divinity School. For a variety of reasons, Yale was his first choice.

> I didn't really want to live in New York City. Of course I had never been to Yale, but I had seen the catalog and I liked the pictures. The campus looked pretty and that's reason enough to go there.

Campbell decided to postpone his seminary education for one year and reapply the next spring. Hoping to improve his transcript, and thus his chances for admission to Yale, he enrolled for a year of graduate study at Tulane University in New Orleans. While at Tulane, he did not pursue a degree, but instead took courses in philosophy, sociology, and labor law. Campbell's labor law professor particularly influenced him, reinforcing his emerging tendency toward social activism. Campbell's social experience at Tulane followed the pattern he set at Wake Forest. "I could not tell you the name of a single person I was in school with." His year at Tulane helped Campbell's record. He reapplied the next year to Yale and was accepted.[61]

Yale appealed to Campbell for more serious reasons than the aesthetics of its catalog. The Divinity School in 1949 had a highly distinguished faculty that attracted many students. Campbell was especially drawn by the work of Liston Pope, a professor of Social Ethics.[62] Pope was the author of *Millhands and Preachers*, a seminal study of the relationship between religion and the textile workers in Gastonia, North Carolina. Himself a Southerner, Pope's social progressivism drew many generations of students to the campus in New Haven. The work of H. Richard Niebuhr, professor of Christian Ethics, also drew Campbell to Yale.[63]

The concern for social activism among young theological liberals also proved a factor in Campbell's attraction to an Ivy League seminary. Campbell recalled many Southerners at the school who were expatriates, hoping to get a grounding in Pope's Social Ethics before they returned to the South.[64] Already, Campbell and these other students saw their time in seminary as a preparation for a career of idealistic social activism, rather than a career of quiet service in a small parish. Campbell recalled that his attraction and that of the other Southerners to Yale Divinity School was the reputation of the school's department of Social Ethics. This discipline was to equip them for addressing the racial problems of the South.[65]

Prominent professors were not the only attraction Yale offered Campbell. Yale provided him a chance to continue his move

---

[61]All information, including the quotations, regarding Campbell's entrance into theological education comes from the author's second interview with Campbell; Dibble interview, 150.

[62]Second interview by author.

[63]Dibble interview, 169.

[64]Caudill interview, 22.

[65]"Our Adolescent History," in *Retrospect: 25 Years of School Desegregation (1954-1979)*, eds. Walter J. Leonard, Robert E. Eaker, and Will D. Campbell, The School Law Symposium Series (Murfreesboro: Middle Tennessee State University, 1979), 40.

beyond the traditional folk religion that originally attracted him to the ministry. Just as Wake Forest provided him a new beginning, Yale Divinity School provided an even more decisive break with his past. Campbell saw the traditional pattern of seminary education among Southern Baptists as a "union card route." By this time, Campbell had no desire to rise to leadership in the denominational structure, and sensed no need for getting an education that would open doors in Southern Baptist life. The military years, as well as his education at Wake Forest and Tulane, had created a new Will Campbell. By this time, he had also rejected puritanical social behavior as the essential element of religion.

> I think probably that was the main reason why I deviated from the pattern of theological education [normally taken by Southern Baptists]. I wanted to go where those things [drinking, dancing, card-playing, etc.] were not the taboos.[66]

Students at Yale enrolled in one of five vocational tracks, according to their ministerial career goal. Each track had a prescribed curriculum preparing a student for parish work, campus ministry, or doctoral studies and teaching. While Campbell's main interest was social activism, he planned at this time to make the local church his base of action. The course of study for parish ministry required extensive training in counseling and pastoral care. Campbell, however, had no interest in those fields, believing them to be little more than courses in "how to hold the blue-veined hand of little old dying Republican men and women." To avoid having "to take all this silly care of the parish," Campbell concentrated in Religion and Higher Education, a major designed for those interested in serving as campus ministers.[67] Even though he did not envision work outside the traditional parish, Campbell's

---

[66]Dibble interview, 169.
[67]Caudill interview, 33.

choice proved wise since he left his first and only pastorate to become a campus minister.

As a student, Campbell's performance at Yale resembled his career at Louisiana College. Good grades were not a high priority for Campbell. An experience in Professor Robert Calhoun's class illustrates his feeling toward his education. One of Campbell's classmates developed a case of conjunctivitis before a major exam and Campbell had volunteered to read to him.

> We were taking our finals our last year . . . when we were supposed to be studying for Calhoun's exam. Calhoun, Robert Calhoun, taught doctrine and was one of the toughest professors on campus. . . . Well, I was reading to this guy because he couldn't, wasn't supposed to read, and so I said I don't want to read any of this shit you know, and I went out and traded cars.[68]

Campbell did have some positive experiences at Yale. He studied Church History under Roland Bainton, the renowned Reformation scholar. Bainton's introduction of Campbell to the Anabaptists gave him a new insight into his own Baptist tradition. However, Campbell remembered that Bainton was the only historian on campus with a positive assessment of the radical reformers. Although Bainton devoted only one or two lectures in his course to Anabaptists, the exposure left a lasting impression on Campbell.[69]

Campbell was also impressed by the person who taught him church polity. Because Yale was an ecumenical divinity school, students were required to take a course in the polity of their respective denomination. These courses were usually taught by area ministers and denomination officials, rather than regular

---

[68]Second interview by author.
[69]Ibid.

faculty.[70] Although Campbell was Baptist, he did not want to take the adjunct professor who taught Baptist polity because he "was a stodgy old Yankee who was very boring." A technicality allowed Campbell to argue his point successfully before the dean, Liston Pope. The professor of Baptist polity was a Northern Baptist (now American Baptist), while Campbell was a Southern Baptist. Campbell protested that he should be able to take a course of his choice since his denominational polity was not offered.

> I told the dean that I was going to take an alien polity, because they don't teach my polity. And he said, "Oh yea, we teach Baptist polity, Mr. Campbell." I said, "Yeah, but that's Northern Baptist, and that's not my denomination." And it wasn't. He said, "What's the difference?" And I told him what I had heard some of my friends say when we were talking about the difference between Southern Baptists and Northern Baptists. . . . [I]t's the difference between a very sick man and a corpse. I never did figure out which was which.

When the dean granted Campbell's request, he chose to take Methodist polity under a teacher who was "fun-loving, [and] full of stories."[71]

Campbell has given mixed responses to his time at Yale. Although he has said at times that he didn't take theological education seriously, at other times he implies that he "did take it seriously and consequently it took me awhile to get over it."[72] Perhaps the two verdicts on his theological education represent his

---

[70]Campbell, third interview by author, Phone call, Nashville, Tennessee, 15 December 1993.

[71]All information regarding the polity course, including the quotations, comes from Second interview by author. In addition, Campbell does not recall the names of either of the adjunct professors who taught polity. The person who taught Methodist polity was an area District Superintendent and the person who taught Baptist polity was a pastor in the area. Campbell, third interview by author.

[72]Caudill interview, 27-28.

assessment from different perspectives. In the immediate context of graduating from seminary, he took his training quite seriously, although his grades were poor. He returned from Yale to the rural South not as a preacher of popular evangelicalism, but as an Ivy League minister. In this regard, he sensed that he cut himself off from his constituency in the interest of sophistication.

In terms of a lasting effect on his religious thought and activism, Campbell has given little credit to Yale. As with Wake Forest and Tulane, Campbell did not make lasting permanent relationships while at Yale. Nor does he feel that his thought was significantly shaped at Yale. "For me to rank the four schools I attended I would put Yale at the very bottom in terms of any lasting impression." Not giving Yale credit for any lasting influence does not mean that he did not have a good experience at the school. Indeed, he had "a very pleasant three years" and in retrospect was "not sorry that I went to Yale Divinity School."[73] What he regrets is that he once equated the erudition that comes with a first-rate education with authentic religion, a view he eventually rejected.

How can one assess Campbell's understanding of his years of higher education? While he does not ascribe a lasting effect of education on his life, Campbell does not give sufficient credit to his own theological education. At Yale he was greatly influenced by Anabaptist thought, many of whose themes surface in several of his novels. This suggest a significant impact of his theological education. His seminary experience also may have shaped him in less tangible ways. Had Campbell taken a more traditional route to the ministry, it is doubtful that he would have been so prone to challenge the status quo. Moreover, it is doubtful that Campbell would have had the literary and theological base to guide both his social activism and his writing without a formal education. Campbell expresses his assessment of his theological education, however, in hyperbole, owing largely to his mature anti-institutionalism. He concedes that formal education can be a

---

[73]Ibid.

necessary preparation for participation in the culture. But he strictly separates cultural values from the values of the community of faith, and he concludes that participation in culture and participation in the community of faith are two different concerns.

Conventional Ministry and the Beginning of Activism

After graduating from Yale in 1952, Campbell was ready to seek employment as a minister. His first two positions were in the mainstream. From 1952 to 1954, he served as pastor of a small church in Louisiana. He left his job as a pastor to take another conventional ministry, Director of Religious Life at the University of Mississippi. After about two years in this position, Campbell took a job that was not a traditional ministry: he became a field director for the Department of Racial and Cultural Relations of the National Council of Churches. While this position was not a traditional ministerial role, the National Council was a mainline organization, and Campbell's role with the organization was hardly radical. Campbell's experience with these three types of ministry—pastor, university chaplain, and ecumenical agent—left him disaffected from institutional religion. Experiences during this time also caused him to reevaluate his motivations for social action. He left the National Council in 1963 to pursue social activism from a more independent—and, in his thinking, more religious—stance.

Taylor, Louisiana is a small town in northern Louisiana, with an economy based on the timber industry. The timber mill in the town was owned by five brothers, three of whom were deacons in the Baptist church. According to the *Louisiana Baptist Convention Annual* of 1953, Taylor Baptist Church had a membership of 275. Under Campbell's leadership, the church added seventeen members through baptism. The new minister appeared eager to contribute to the congregation's growth.[74] Traditional growth was not the only concern of the Ivy League graduate. Campbell arrived in the town in 1952, eager to educate these traditional church members away from what he thought was their narrow biblicism.[75]

He was equally eager to put to use the lessons of his Social Ethics classes. At first, he wanted to decline a salary from the church and seek employment in the mill. While some in the congregation had mild support for the idea, the mill owners strongly discouraged him from doing so. Apparently knowing of Campbell's sympathy for labor unions, the mill owners' reservations presented Campbell with something of a threat.[76] While he declined to be so vocal in Taylor, Campbell found another site where he could voice his concerns. In a labor strike in the town of Elizabeth, two-hundred miles away, Campbell spoke to the workers in a rally and marched on the picket line. When news of his actions were reported in the major north Louisiana newspaper, the churchfolk were unusually tolerant, although they clearly lacked sympathy for his causes.[77]

His pastorate was not geared toward social activism alone, however. The new minister also poured himself into some of the traditional ministerial roles. He worked with the youth of the church, and started an innovative approach to children's summer programs. Instead of the traditional one-week Vacation Bible School, Campbell organized a day camp that lasted six weeks.[78] He also joined the Lions Club in an effort to fulfill some of the standard roles as a community leader.[79] In many ways, then, Campbell believed that he was performing the traditional roles of a small-town minister.

------

[74]Louisiana Baptist Convention, *Annual of the Louisiana Baptist Convention* (Baton Rouge: Louisiana State Convention, 1953), 132.

[75]Caudill interview, 28. "[T]hese people can't go on believing that a fish swallowed a man."

[76]Second interview by author.

[77]Caudill interview, 30-32.

[78]Ibid.

[79]"Our Adolescent History," 40-41.

Looking back on those days, he thought of himself as "a dandy little preacher," which he came to equate with being "the mascot" under control of the members.[80] His wife, Brenda, enjoyed the traditional role of the pastor's wife even less. She was often asked to play the piano, which she declined.

> She did sing in the choir a little bit, but . . . she pretty soon let them know that I'm not going to be at all of the WMU meetings and that you hired my husband, you didn't hire me.[81]

He fulfilled these roles out of obligation, hoping that by engaging in some traditional roles, he would have an avenue to influence the congregation on his social concerns. Campbell discovered, to his dismay, that the social messages in his sermons neither persuaded the members, nor enraged them. His words were ignored. A leading church matron stopped him one day to let him know how unaffected they were. Evidently, Campbell frequently addressed the race issue and the anti-communist scare from the pulpit. Miss Rosalie told him that all the ministers in the church had a "pet subject" that they dwelt on, but she had noticed that Campbell had two: "McCarthyism and the Negro question."[82] The conversation left the impression on Campbell that the community was at best amused, and at worst, unaffected by his actions.

Indeed, when the Supreme Court handed down the landmark *Brown v. Board of Education* ruling, Campbell noticed that the community was not initially frightened. He was attending a meeting of the Lions Club when the Court announced its ruling, and he recalled that the local superintendent promised that the ruling would be ignored.[83] When Campbell told the congregation that the ruling meant that black and white children would

---

[80]Second interview by author.
[81]Ibid.
[82]Ibid.
[83]"Our Adolescent History," 40-41.

eventually go to the same school, the church leadership "found it kind of cute."

> They kind of delighted in going to the club and saying that our little preacher is the cutest thing. He talks about our children going to school with darkies, isn't that cute? And he went to Yale and got corrupted, but he's going to be alright.[84]

When Campbell left the church, he did so more out of frustration than out of fear of losing his job. Many in the church "were sorry to see us go," he recalled.[85] The community, however, in the months after *Brown* gradually became more realistic about the implications of the decision. For his part, Campbell believed that increasing awareness on their part meant that a clash of beliefs was inevitable if he remained. Sensing a mounting frustration among the members, he decided to leave.[86] He did not leave, however, with the sense that he was running from the problem. The fact that the congregation at first was amused and then somewhat angry had left Campbell feeling that his presence in the community served no lasting purpose. Disillusioned with the efficacy of mere preaching, he came to believe that, "The only way to teach anybody is precept and example. . . . the pulpit, that's probably the poorest way to communicate with a congregation." After about two years of communicating through this "poor medium," Campbell decided to move to a position he felt was more promising: university work.

Campbell's decision to leave his position with Taylor Baptist Church was more than a desire to move to a new church. It was a desire to leave the pastorate. His eighteen months at the church left him feeling that he could not "survive in the traditional parish ministry." He was not, however, ready to leave the ministry.

---

[84]Ibid.
[85]Caudill interview, 31.
[86]Second interview by author.

Rather, he wanted a position that was less conventional than the pastorate. His decision in divinity school to avoid the curriculum track for parish ministry had then kept him away from undesirable courses. Now, his earlier choice would help him move into a position as a college chaplain.

Campbell reactivated his placement file at Yale and soon received two offers, one at the University of Oklahoma and one at the University of Mississippi. Although friends advised him to take the Oklahoma job, a desire to return to his native state pulled him to Ole Miss.[87] He thought the campus environment would not only be different from the pastorate, it would be more open. He arrived in Oxford, Mississippi in 1954 with plans to make it his lifetime home.[88] He left after two hectic years, a far more controversial figure than he ever was at Taylor.

The University of Mississippi is located in the northern Mississippi town of Oxford, about ninety miles south of Memphis. Founded in 1848, the school was the first public institution of higher education in the state. Although academically strong, Campbell's new place of employment had seen its share of hardship. The school closed during the Civil War when all the students left to enlist in the Confederate Army. During the late 1920s, Governor Theodore Bilbo removed the school's administration and essentially took control of the school. Bilbo's actions were part of a larger effort to merge all the state colleges and universities into a single institution in Jackson. The relocation effort failed, and Bilbo's heavy-handed actions cost the university its accreditation for two years.[89]

The school's greatest infamy later became James Meredith's 1962 attempt to enroll as the first African American at the school.

---

[87]"Southernness" and a sense of place play a strong role in Campbell's self-awareness and in his thought. For a more detailed discussion, see Chapter Four, below.

[88]Caudill interview, 29, 33-34.

[89]Charles Reagan Wilson and William Ferris, eds., *Encyclopedia of Southern Culture* (Chapel Hill: University of North Carolina Press, 1988), s.v. "The University of Mississippi," by David Sansing.

Though by that time, *Brown v. Board of Education* was eight years old, public education in most of the Deep South was still segregated. Missisissippi had accordingly made no move toward desegregation. In fact, public institutions had made every effort to avoid integration. Meredith's enrollment was part of an effort to force the university into compliance with the law. Despite the governor's efforts to bar his admission and the rioting that required federal troops to restore order, Meredith eventually became a student at the school.[90]

A decade before James Meredith clashed with the University of Mississippi, Will D. Campbell challenged the social mores of segregation at the school. Although Campbell's confrontation was less violent, it foreshadowed the Meredith incident. In some regards, Campbell's work at the school in the 1950s served as a prelude to the violent 1960s.

When Campbell assumed his position at the school, the *Brown* decision was new and largely untested. The response to *Brown* in Mississippi differed little from that of Taylor, as Campbell recalled. In the 1950s, integration was not yet feared, it was disbelieved. Most people, according to Campbell, simply did not think that institutions once limited to whites would have the two races working side by side.[91] To the contrary, Campbell intended to make the campus aware of the implications of *Brown* and to do his part to apply the rulings of the case to the university.

One of the first things Campbell did was to promote integration through his personal actions. Many of his actions directly rejected the standard protocol governing the relations between whites and blacks. Among his first brazen acts was a trip to an interracial cooperative farm in Holmes County, several hours away

---

[90]Ibid. See also James A. Cabaniss, *A History of the University of Mississippi: Its First Hundred Years*, 2nd ed. (Hattiesburg: University College Press of Mississippi, 1971). James Silver, *Mississippi: The Closed Society*, new ed. (New York: Harcourt, Brace, and World, 1966) gives a personal analysis of the crisis that arose from the effort to enroll James Meredith. Silver was a history professor at the school, and a friend of Campbell while he was at the university.

[91]*Brother to a Dragonfly*, 108.

from Oxford. Providence Farm was founded in the 1930s by a group of religious social activists under the influence of Sherwood Eddy, Kirby Page, and Reinhold Niebuhr. Operating out of a world view of Christian Socialism, these men inspired the creation of this farm, which originally served as a cotton cooperative farmed by evicted sharecroppers and tenants. Providence also gave economic assistance to the poor by providing credit unions and cooperative purchasing.

Providence was twenty years old when Campbell first heard about its programs. The farm had operated in relative obscurity for most of its history, and its goal of creating a worker-run cotton cooperative failed. The free medical clinic, on the other hand, continued to operate. By the 1950s, Providence was essentially a small clinic offering health care to the poor people of the area.[92] In the emerging hysteria of the civil rights crisis, however, even a clinic offering free health care was not be immune from attack. Several months before Campbell's visit to the farm, two men kidnapped and murdered a fourteen year old AfricanAmerican, Emmett Till, because he spoke to a white woman "in a familiar manner," violating the traditional norm of social distance between the races. The murder's aftermath created fear throughout the state that social segregation was under siege. Many people decided to take any means necessary to preserve traditional racial arrangements.[93]

---

[92]Caudill interview, 37; *Providence* (Atlanta: Longstreet Press, 1992), 2-7. Campbell's attraction to the work of these men probably grew out of his commitment to social activism. He did not cite any of these men as being particularly influential on the development of his beliefs. While Campbell's appreciation of the idea of corporate sin came at a later point, the work of Reinhold Niebuhr received no credit. The thought of Karl Barth and Jacques Ellul have figured more prominently in Campbell's own religious world view.

[93]David R. Goldfield, *Black, White, and Southern: Race Relations and Southern Culture* (Baton Rouge: Louisiana State University Press, 1990), 88-89; Stephen J. Whitfield, *A Death in the Delta: The Story of Emmett Till* (New York: The Free Press, 1988).

Some time after the Till murder, an incident in another Mississippi community seemed to challenge traditional race relations. Four African-American teens were arrested after a white girl in the third grade became frightened, thinking the young boys had threatened her. What happened was not clear, but where it happened was definite—almost in sight of Providence Farm.

When news of the incident spread in the community, the obscure farm suddenly became the subject of mass animosity by many of the local whites. Many community leaders demanded that the farm be shut. Hearing of the conflict on regional and national media reports, Campbell decided to travel to Holmes County to see the operations of Providence Farm firsthand.

Campbell traveled to the farm with G. McLeod Bryan, a professor at Mercer University who was delivering a series of lectures at the University of Mississippi. When they arrived at Providence, Bryan introduced Campbell to Eugene and Lindy Cox, and David and Sue Minter. These two couples had come to the farm prompted by their religious convictions to do social work. After their meeting, Campbell and Bryan left the farm late in the evening to return to Oxford. At the end of the road outside the farm, the sheriff and several citizens had set up a roadblock, apparently to add to the mounting pressure to close Providence. Minter agreed to drive Campbell's car to the roadblock, thinking that his presence at the wheel would ease Campbell and Bryan through. The men passed through the roadblock without incident, but one of the guards copied the license tag number. The next morning, Campbell was summoned to the administration building.[94]

Administrators told Campbell that the sheriff of Holmes County ran a check on the license and discovered that the car's owner was an employee of the University of Mississippi. That discovery set a chain of events in motion. The sheriff of Holmes County contacted the sheriff who had jurisdiction over the

---

[94]*Providence*, 2-7, 14-20, 24. For a detailed discussion of other aspects of Campbell's relationship with Providence Farm, see Chapter Four, below.

university. Then, Campbell's superiors were contacted. An administrator told Campbell that

> The state senator from Holmes County was on the campus
> . . . and said he wants to know what the hell one of our
> men was doing in Holmes County last night. . . . [Campbell
> replied] I launched into this sophonic [sic] tirade. "Yes, I
> was in Holmes County. . . . I was down there visiting some
> Christian missionaries. . . . [N]ot only was I there but I'm
> going back Sunday afternoon."[95]

According to Campbell, that incident was his first conflict with the university.[96]

The furor over Campbell's trip to Providence Farm was mild compared to his next challenge to the school. He believed the time had come to force the university community to come to terms with the implications of *Brown*. Whether the school opposed integration or embraced it, Campbell wanted to see that the school did not ignore it. Religious Emphasis Week provided the occasion.

Religious Emphasis Week was an innocuous annual event started by Campbell's predecessor. The week was often called, "Be Good to God Week." Speakers were chosen ostensibly by a student-member Committee of One Hundred, but in reality the Committee merely approved the choice of the Director of Religious Life. Campbell's choice of speakers insured that the week would be far from innocuous. Since the university ignored the race issue, Campbell planned to select speakers who were outspoken in support of integration.[97] What the week was to be, in fact, was a symposium on the race issue.

---

[95]Caudill interview, 40.
[96]Ibid., 41.
[97]*Brother to a Dragonfly*, 113.

I loaded it and meant to load it. . . . Every waking moment,
every breath, everything was revolving around that issue,
that question [race].[98]

Because supporters of integration were scarce in Mississippi,
Campbell could choose some activists without the public discover-
ing his agenda beforehand. The speakers for the February event
were chosen in the fall semester. All those confirmed for the
meeting were involved in some manner in the nascent civil rights
movement. Joe Elmore, a classmate of Campbell's from Yale, was
invited. Francis Pickens Miller, a political activist from Virginia
who had almost unseated the segregationist Senator Harry Byrd,
agreed to come. The Presbyterian minister at Monticello, Mississippi, George Chauncy, also a classmate of Campbell's, was on the
program. A prominent rabbi from Birmingham, Milton Grafman
accepted the engagement. The Jesuit sociologist, Joseph Fichter, a
professor at Loyola of New Orleans, also confirmed for the week.
Finally, a formerly obscure priest from Ohio was to speak.[99]

Alvin Kershaw was a jazz-playing Episcopal priest who had a
brief moment of fame when he appeared on the televised game-
show, "The $64,000 Question." Winning $32,000, Kershaw
stopped playing and announced that he would give his winnings to
charity. The combination of musical talent and philanthropy was
sure to draw a crowd. Unfortunately for Campbell's plans, the
philanthropy drew the suspicions of some of the state's reactionary
journalists. One of Kershaw's designated charities was the NAACP,
a fact which the media soon exposed.[100]

Pressure from all sectors was brought to bear on Campbell to
withdraw the invitation to Kershaw. Although the university
administrators led in creating pressure on Campbell, they were
actually responding to pressure placed on them by the governor
and many state legislators. The conflict dragged on for four

---

[98]Caudill interview, 42.
[99]Ibid., 43.
[100]*Brother to a Dragonfly*, 114.

months, with Campbell refusing to remove Kershaw. His excuse was that the students, not he, had invited Kershaw.[101] Meanwhile, Campbell traveled to Ohio to meet with Kershaw and develop a contingency plan. Should Kershaw's invitation be withdrawn, the other speakers would refuse to come. The plan was developed with the assistance of the Southern Regional Council. Founded in 1944, the Southern Regional Council was an organization led by progressive white Southerners committed to improving race relations. The organization initially worked to improve the plight of African America ns without challenging the concept of "separate but equal." By the 1950s, however, the Council openly advocated integration and purposed to help create change in the white community. With this goal in mind the Council provided support to whites like Campbell who challenged segregation.[102]

From the time the invitation to Kershaw was announced in October, 1955 until the meeting was scheduled to open on February 19, 1956, the administration and the political leadership of the state pressured Campbell to withdraw the invitation. Just before the initial meeting, matters came to a head.[103] About midnight one evening in February, Campbell was visiting at the home of history professor James Silver, himself a challenger to many of the school's racial standards. A security officer found Campbell there and summoned him to the Chancellor's home.[104] When Campbell arrived, he found a room full of men who had just concluded an emergency meeting to resolve the confusion sur-rounding Religious Emphasis Week. Several administrators voiced

---

[101]Caudill interview, 43-44.

[102]*Brother to a Dragonfly*, 115. See also Wilson and Ferris, eds., *Encyclopedia of Southern Culture*, s.v. "Southern Regional Council," by Anthony Newberry, 1425-1426.

[103]Milton Bracker, "Mississippi Parley on Religion Periled by Ban on Minister," *New York Times*, 11 February 1956, 1 and 38; Bracker, "Mississippi Plans a Religious Week," *New York Times*, 12 February 1956, 86.

[104]Silver was forced from the university a decade later after actively supporting the enrollment of James Meredith. See James Silver, *Running Scared: Silver in Mississippi* (Jackson: University Press of Mississippi, 1984).

their opinions as to why Kershaw should not appear. The Chancellor concluded the meeting and the issue with the words, "The man can't come. Whatever it takes, he can't come to the campus. . . . Let's word a telegram. Will, we'd like for you to stay if you like."[105]

The prearranged plan for all the other speakers to cancel quickly began operation. Each speaker informed the university that he would not participate in the week's activities because the school had canceled Kershaw's invitation. Campbell was especially concerned about Francis Miller of Virginia and Rabbi Milton Grafman of Alabama. Eventually these two withdrew as well. Declining to appear was especially hard for Grafman because he and the Chancellor were personal friends.[106] In the end, social concern prevailed over friendship and the rabbi remained in Birmingham.

The administration of the university developed a contingency plan to prevent a disaster. The Chancellor planned to ask local ministers to replace those speakers who backed out of the engagement. At first, the plan looked potentially successful. In that event, any lesson Campbell hoped to present to the community would be lost. Indeed, the race issue would continue to be ignored if the speakers could cancel with so little disruption to the flow of the conference. Campbell contacted Neil Joffrion, the minister of the Episcopal Church, asking him to encourage the local ministers to boycott the meeting. Joffrion successfully persuaded all the ministers to reject the university's invitations.[107] Campbell later recalled:

---

[105]*Brother to a Dragonfly*, 120. Campbell did not approve of the telegram, but he was resigned to the fact that Kershaw's dismissal was inevitable. For this reason, he did not give a strong protest to sending a telegram. Asked if he approved of the wording, he said "Yes, it's all right with me. If you are going to send the telegram, I don't care what you say." When the Chancellor and Campbell had to appear before the campus chapter of the American Association of University Professors, the Chancellor was able to say that Campbell "concurred" with the decision. See Caudill interview, 46.

[106]Caudill interview, 49.

[107]*Brother to a Dragonfly*, 121.

[Joffrion] handled the local clergy and they declined. . . . To a man! They declined to come, including the Baptist. All of them declined to come across the picket line. . . . It was difficult for them, and particularly the Methodist man who was the chancellor's pastor.[108]

When the time for Religious Emphasis Week arrived, Campbell had the moral victory. Although his original program had been canceled, Campbell had succeeded in preventing the administration from developing a substitute program. In effect, Campbell still controlled the week. Each day when the sessions had been scheduled, Campbell sat in silence in the auditorium, filled with hundreds of sympathetic supporters.

Religious Emphasis Week marked the beginning of the end for Campbell at the University of Mississippi. Before he resigned, however, Campbell continued to challenge the segregated world view of the community and devised a plan to facilitate the integration of the school. He encouraged an African American to enroll in a correspondence course offered by the university. At first, his plan was intended as no more than a joke. Soon, Campbell and the African-American, a young local minister, began to see it as a serious move. Correspondence courses did not require one to appear in person to register. If the man could successfully enroll, the incident would mean that the school had broken the color barrier.

After Campbell and the man discussed the idea in Campbell's office, they stopped in the lobby to play ping-pong. This action proved to be a greater challenge to the prevailing social values than the minister's enrollment. The two were spotted by a law student and a staff member, both of whom were segregationists. When the game was over, Campbell drove the minister back to his home and returned to the campus, where the two men confronted him about having such close social relations with a member of another race.

---

[108]Caudill interview, 50.

The entire confrontation eventually resulted in a meeting with the Dean of Student Personnel.

> I tried to quiet the Dean when he called me in about the ping-pong game by telling him that it was really quite within the Southern pattern. We had used separate but equal paddles, the ball was white, and there was net drawn tightly between us.

The next day the Campbell family arose to a front yard filled with ping-pong balls painted white and black.

In the aftermath of the ping-pong game one final act of harassment remained for Campbell. He hosted a party for new students on campus. During the course of the evening, someone placed human feces covered with powdered sugar in the punch, obviously a crude comment on Campbell's one-man campaign to desegregate the school. Compounding the injury was the university's failure, in Campbell's estimation, to investigate the incident.[109] The punch bowl incident strained his patience to the breaking point. Almost twenty years later, he said, "I just couldn't adjust to fecal punch."[110] Reading the writing on the wall, Campbell decided his usefulness at the campus had been exhausted and that it was time to move on.

Campbell's supporters on the university faculty—historian James Silver, political scientist Huey Blair Howerton, and William H. Willis of the Department of Classics—believed that his presence put some needed pressure on the university that would be ended by his departure. They hoped, in vain, to persuade him to stay. Not only was he tired of the harassment but also he had received an offer from the National Council of Churches to work full-time in race relations.[111] It was a good time to move.

---

[109]*Brother to a Dragonfly*, 121, 126-127.
[110]"Good Will," *Newsweek*, 8 May 1972, 84.
[111]*Brother to a Dragonfly*, 128.

Campbell left the University of Mississippi with mixed feelings. Although he was not fired, he nonetheless had a sense of being forced from his job, and he doubted that his contract would have been renewed when it expired. He moved away "with a sense of tragedy" because he enjoyed much about working at the school in spite of his clashes with authority. He also saw tragedy in the unfinished work of integration. Yet, he also completed his tenure at the university "with a sense of satisfaction that I had dramatized a truth in a university setting which I thought was important."[112]

The National Council of Churches had a long heritage of social activism. Founded in 1950, the NCC was an ecumenical agency directly descended from the earlier work of the Evangelical Alliance and the Federal Council of Churches of Christ in America. Both of these agencies had strongly advocated social action.[113] Although most conservative, sectarian denominations did not affiliate with the NCC, all the mainline churches became part of this movement, and in the 1950s mainline denominationalism constituted the vanguard of Protestantism.

From the beginning, the NCC had interests that extended far beyond building bridges between denominations. This ecumenical agency set out to help create a socially progressive agenda. By the time the civil rights movement was in full force in the 1960s, the NCC represented one of the strongest voices of support within the white community.[114]

Much of the work in support of Civil Rights came from the NCC's Division of Racial and Cultural Relations. This Division was the heir to the Federal Council's Department of Race Rela-

---

[112]Caudill interview, 52-53.

[113]Daniel Reid, et al., eds. *Dictionary of Christianity in America* (Downers Grove, Illinois: Intervarsity Press, 1990), s.v. "National Council of Churches of Christ in the U.S.A.," by P. A. Crow.

[114]For an excellent discussion of the role of the NCC in the civil rights movement, see James Findlay, Jr., *Church People in the Struggle: The National Council of Churches and the Black Freedom Movement, 1950-1970* (New York: Oxford University Press, 1993). Findlay discusses Campbell's role with the NCC. See 23-27.

tions, founded in 1921. The leaders of the Division took a cautious approach to race relations, emphasizing education and slow change. The increasing violence directed against African Americans motivated the organization to change tactics in the 1950s. Under its director, J. Oscar Lee, the Division decided to establish a Southern office with a field director who would take a more direct role in race relations.[115] Campbell and the job seemed made for each other.

In effect Campbell was "sort of a trouble-shooter" for the NCC and for civil rights activists. He traveled to various sites where civil rights activities resulted in violence or were likely to do so. Campbell's role was technically that of an advisor. He was not to participate in marches directly. Rather, his presence was to lend moral support to the participants, especially when they were arrested and placed in jail because of their activities. Campbell had one other function as an observer. If an African American were arrested on a serious charge in relation with a protest or wished to bring charges against someone, the testimony was not likely to be taken seriously by the court. Campbell's presence insured that a white man could testify on behalf of the injured or in defense of the accused. The NCC hoped that his presence would lessen the chances of any unfair legal hearings.[116]

The national office of the NCC was in New York, but the leaders allowed Campbell to choose the location of his field office. His experiences at the University of Mississippi eliminated that state as an option. Finally, he settled on Nashville both because it was urban and because its location was central to most of the southland. Campbell made a wise choice by selecting Nashville: his first involvements were very close to the city. In 1956, he traveled to hot spots in Sturgis and Clay, Kentucky.

The year 1957 was equally momentous for Campbell. He traveled to Little Rock, Arkansas, in anticipation of the court-ordered desegregation of the public schools. Campbell escorted the

[115]Findlay, 18-20.
[116]*Brother to a Dragonfly*, 128; *Forty Acres and a Goat*, 78.

young African American students through the angry mob, and returned several times before the end of the school year. He also traveled to the east Tennessee town of Clinton, the sight of an unusual amount of violence instigated by the Ku Klux Klan. Campbell hoped to encourage the pastor of the First Baptist Church to take a stand in support of integration.[117]

That same year, Campbell traveled to the first meeting of the Southern Christian Leadership Conference. Attendance at the meeting was momentous not only because it was the organizational meeting but also because he was the only white person present. As Campbell recalled, the meeting was modest in many regards, including the various resolutions that were passed. Most of the meeting's position papers were mere calls for the inclusion of African Americans in the economic life of the nation. The meeting was bold, however, in its approach to the white community. The SCLC aimed to be a movement led by African Americans for African Americans. In Campbell's estimation, the new organization welcomed white support, but not white leadership. Even benevolent leadership was beginning to be seen as paternalistic.[118]

The year 1957 also brought Campbell into involvement with efforts to desegregate Nashville businesses and schools. The school board of Nashville had approved a plan to desegregate the schools gradually. Called "the Nashville plan," it stipulated that the school system would desegregate one grade per year over a twelve year period. Campbell worked closely with African American minister Kelly Miller Smith, whose daughter was one of the first to attend an integrated school. Despite the moderate, even conservative tone of the plan, violence met many of its advocates.[119]

The next years continued to bring opportunities to participate directly in the growing movement. Campbell worked closely with the Student Interracial Ministry, established in the 1960s under the leadership of Union Theological Seminary. This program was

---

[117]Ibid., 55, 63.
[118]"Our Adolescent History," 62.
[119]*Forty Acres and a Goat*, 50-51.

designed to place black students in white churches and white students in black churches for a summer internship.[120]

He also contributed to efforts to desegregate the restaurants of Nashville. Restaurateurs of the city were especially resistant to change. Not only did many of them personally oppose integration but also those who might have considered desegregating their facilities were faced with the threat of losing their clientele. Many of the sit-ins at lunch counters across the South were led by African American students, and Nashville was no exception. Nashville was also no exception to the violence that plagued the lunch counter sit-ins. Before the first round of sit-ins, Campbell negotiated a plan with a leading owner of a local restaurant. The owner said he would voluntarily serve African American customers if the protesters would not picket his restaurant. He would serve several African Americans, discretely and without drama, and then use his influence in the local restaurant association to have that organization come out in favor of integrated facilities. The plan was certain to have worked, but an error in communication among the demonstrators on the day of the protest brought picketers in front of the restaurant. In reaction the owner rescinded his offer to serve the students. The protesters marched into various lunch counters around the city of Nashville, led by such young students as Diane Nash, Marion Barry, and John Lewis.[121]

Campbell's work with the NCC also brought him into contact with the Kennedy administration. The young president, developing an interest in the growing move for racial justice across the South, asked his brother, Robert, the U. S. Attorney General, to initiate some limited involvement. Campbell and a group of white social activists met with Robert Kennedy in Washington, and Campbell remained in contact with them for several years. The meeting was essentially "cordial." Kennedy, however, refused to believe Campbell's suggestion that FBI agents "native to" the South were often

---

[120]Ibid., 30, 41.
[121]Ibid., 71-79, 90-91.

more sympathetic with local law enforcement agencies than they were with the safety of the protesters.[122]

By 1962 Campbell had worked for the NCC for eight years, the longest length of time he had held a single position. At first, this position seemed to have been the job that would allow him to engage in faith-based social action on his own terms. He eventually came to feel, however, that the NCC as an institutional structure was as restrictive as his first two positions of ministry. A first change in this direction came in Campbell's involvement with a civil rights demonstration at Albany, Georgia. The Albany Campaign brought hundreds of northern protesters to this southern town. Protest leaders had arranged to have bail posted immediately following the arrests of demonstrators, after which they would leave the city and return to their homes. Campbell and Andrew Young, an associate of Martin Luther King and director of Field Foundation funded Citizenship school, had the task of posting bail. Young, however, deliberately delayed posting the bail until after the Sheriff's office had closed for the day. Apparently he thought, as Campbell would come to believe, that many of these activists did not understand the complexity and personal sacrifice required to make the protests work. To be arrested and be immediately bailed out of jail was too sanitized a procedure, and it was a luxury that local African Americans did not have.[123]

The Albany Movement's massive arrests increased national awareness of southern racial patterns. For Campbell, the event was a turning point of a different sort. For the first time, he began to see the white Southerner, especially the working class Southerner, as a victim. The sheriff in Albany was named Laurie Pritchett. Pritchett did not match the stereotype of the southern sheriff that brought fear into so many protesters. Pritchett was a Southern Baptist who was attending catechism to become a Roman Catholic, and evidently a gentle man.

---

[122]*Brother to a Dragonfly*, 131-135.
[123]Andrew Young, *An Easy Burden: The Civil Rights Movement and the Transformation of America* (New York: Harper Collins, 1996), 164-184.

According to Campbell's description, Pritchett treated the demonstrators with a certain amount of respect, removing his hat when they began praying as part of the demonstration.[124] When Campbell wrote his alternative description of the Albany Movement for *The Christian Century*, he was seen as not fully sympathetic with the protesters. Moreover, Campbell could no longer demonize all the whites who were not sympathetic toward the demonstrations.[125]

Campbell's break with the NCC, however, came from his involvement with the National Conference on Religion and Race, held in 1962 in Chicago. The Conference was a gathering of the nation's major Jewish and Christian leaders, convened to impress further upon the nation's churches the importance of taking a stand for integration. Speakers included Abraham Heschel, Sargent Shriver, and Martin Luther King, Jr., as well as the forceful William Stringfellow. Campbell was also scheduled to speak. In the "advance copy" Campbell sent to the New York office, his speech reflected his strongly religious approach to racial issues. Campbell felt that the civil rights movement, as a religious movement, had not expressed an adequate doctrine of original sin. While social activists were eager to express an optimistic view of humanity, they were less eager to accept the potential for evil posed by all humans. In his speech, Campbell planned to say,

> If I live to be as old as my father I expect to see whites marched into the gas chambers, the little children clutching their toys to their breasts in Auschwitz fashion, at the hands of a black Eichmann.[126]

---

[124]*Brother to a Dragonfly*, 164-168.

[125]"Perhaps; and Maybe," *The Christian Century*, 19 September 1962, 1133. "So that article got a little criticism that I was being sympathetic. I had referred to him [the sheriff] as a good man. . . . [People missed the irony of my comments.] The Pharisees were good people." Caudill interview, 69.

[126]*Brother to a Dragonfly*, 229-230.

Conference officials demanded that Campbell delete the words from the actual delivery of his speech. The original version, however, had already been distributed to the news media. When Campbell reached the objectionable words in his text, he did not merely omit them in his delivery. He stood for a moment of silence while the audience read the unspoken words. His point had been made, despite the objections of his employers. While this provocative, unspoken segment of his speech angered many present, other proposals in his speech were more indicative of a social progressive. Campbell called for expanding the civil rights struggle to include full integration of housing, voter registration and education, scholarships for minorities to attend predominately white schools, and the continuation of the Student Interracial Ministry.[127] While many people at the conference were angered at Campbell's assessment of the universality of human sin, Mississippi newspapers reported instead that a native son had advocated complete social integration.[128] In Campbell's attempt to be consistent, he was now consistently offending everyone.

When Campbell first went to work for the NCC, the job appealed to him in part because it allowed him to pursue his interests in religiously-oriented social activism with little interference. "I was in Nashville," he recalled, "and the National Council was in New York. They didn't know what I was doing and they didn't know what to tell me to do."[129] By the time he displayed some sympathy toward Laurie Pritchett in Albany and reminded conference attendees in Chicago about the human potential for evil, the national office had become aware of Campbell's world

---

[127]"The Inner Life of Church and Synagogue," in *Race: Challenge to Religion*, ed. Mathew Ahman (Chicago: Henry Regnery Company, 1963), 22-24. This volume contained several of the speeches given at the conference, including Campbell's speech minus the "Eichmann" comment.

[128]Ibid. Although the media often has a reputation for socially progressive views, the leading newspapers in Mississippi actively supported the maintenance of segregation. See John Ray Skates, *Mississippi: A Bicentennial History* (New York: W.W. Norton and Company, 1979), 159.

[129]Second interview by author,

view and was increasingly uncomfortable with his approach. His immediate supervisor was "never too happy . . . with the approach I was taking."[130]

Now, the national organization wished to place tighter constraints on their field director. His superiors ordered Campbell to submit all future articles and speeches for approval.

> Of course I refused. No one had asked me to do that when I worked for the state of Mississippi and I would not do it for what was supposed to be the most liberal and free organization in the nation.[131]

This restriction by the national office resulted in Campbell's resignation by the end of the year. The incident also aided Campbell in realizing that, from his perspective, his starting point for social activism was more sectarian than that of the mainline churches. Campbell was asked to evaluate his understanding of his job duties. From his perspective, he was a minister at large. The NCC, he thought, wanted him to be "a social engineer."

> Well, what are you [they asked]? I said I am a preacher. They said that by charter we cannot pay a person to preach. We are not—the National Council has no theology. I said, "Oh, yeah, you have a theology, alright, you just have a piss-poor one." That is a theological statement in itself.[132]

Although painful, the experience also caused him to re-examine his approach to social activism. After this Campbell developed an anti-institutional perspective toward social structures. Institutions, from Campbell's view, were self-serving and motivated ultimately by

---

[130]Caudill interview, 65.

[131]"Vocation as Grace," in *Callings*, eds. Will D. Campbell and James Y. Holloway (New York: Paulist Press, 1974), 274.

[132]Second interview by author.

self-preservation, regardless of their ideology. In the final analysis, according to Campbell, any institution, liberal or conservative, is motivated more by its own need to preserve itself than by any altruism it may espouse. "In my experiences," he has argued, "[institutions are] all after your soul, your ultimate allegiance, and they get it one way or another or you're out."[133] While it had a different set of rules, "the channel one was expected to swim in [with the NCC] was really no wider than Taylor, Louisiana . . . or Oxford, Mississippi."[134]

In retrospect, Campbell considered the restrictions of the liberal sector to be worse than others. These feelings grew out of the fact that his disillusionment with the NCC was greater than what he experienced in the previous two positions. He went to the NCC with high ideals, but at the end of his employment he did not "really see any more sympathy for opposing positions. . . . They're just as impatient and make fun of people who differ with them—you know one way of burning the heretics is to make fun of them."[135] When Campbell left the NCC, he had worked in three types of institutional ministry, and had been disappointed in all three. He complained:

> This flight from local parish to the enlightenment of the academy to the promised land of an ecumenical council had been a journey to nowhere.[136]

By 1963, Campbell left the NCC, never again to be employed by a conventional ministry. He did not, however, cease to speak out on significant social issues. Some of his supporters approved of

---

[133]Ibid.

[134]*Brother to a Dragonfly*, 130.

[135]Second interview by author.

[136]*Forty Acres and a Goat*, 6. Campbell did not deny the positive role of the NCC in social activism. It was the utopian approach of the NCC to social problems that he opposed. "I think the National Council of Churches . . . did some, some good things in the sixties, in the racial crisis. They were the only ones [of the white churches] to address the crisis." Second interview by author.

his independent approach to social activism and wanted him to continue, even though he no longer had an employer. These people secured control of the Fellowship of Southern Churchmen, an organization that was defunct by the 1960s, but that had a grand heritage of social activism. The Fellowship was organized in Monteagle, Tennessee by James Dombrowski and Howard Kester. Their chief interest lay in labor reform, and by the 1950s, the group had largely spent its energy.[137]

Technically, the group was still in existence in 1964, with a valid tax exemption number as a non-profit organization. Because Reinhold Niebuhr was involved in the creation of the Fellowship, the organization was "roughly in the Neo-Orthodox to liberal school theologically," which made Campbell comfortable. The group under Campbell was renamed the Committee of Southern Churchmen, and it became a much less structured organization than the Fellowship. The new organization was changed from a membership organization to a board organization, hence the name, "Committee." The new group did not solicit members, reflecting Campbell's disdain for organizations and his desire to live consistently with that view.

Indeed, the main purpose of the Committee was to provide Campbell a salary. The group did not have the comprehensive goals of the Fellowship since it was actually "intended to be nothing more than a front for my [Campbell's] work. . . . It's a vehicle."[138] In his assessment of the new organization, he said, "It was nothing. It was a name and a tax exemption and whatever I and a few other people were doing on a given day."

---

[137] Samuel Hill, *Encyclopedia of Southern Religion*, s.v. "Fellowship of Southern Churchmen," by Anthony Dunbar. See also Robert Martin, "Critique of Southern Society and Vision of a New Order: The Fellowship of Southern Churchmen, 1934-1957," *Church History* 52 (1983): 66-80; and Anthony Dunbar, *Against the Grain: Southern Radicals and Prophets, 1929-1959* (Charlottesville: University Press of Virginia, 1981).
[138] Dibble interview, 158.

The most structured thing the group did was publish a magazine from 1965 until 1983.[139] The group decided to name the magazine *Katallagete*, which is the Greek imperative, "be reconciled," used in II Corinthians 2: 5, 20. They chose this unusual name in order to highlight the message that the human community has been reconciled or restored to communion with God.[140]

In addition to Campbell the Committee of Southern Churchmen included the likes of Jim Holloway, a professor at Berea College in Kentucky, who served as editor of *Katallagete*, Baptists Joseph Hendricks of Mercer University, G. McLeod Bryan of Wake Forest University, and Kelly Smith, Campbell's longtime ally in Nashville. Joining these men were James McBride Dabbs, a Presbyterian layman; Andrew Lipscomb, a minister from Georgia; and Walker Percy, the author and active Roman Catholic layman. Thomas Merton, the Trappist monk from Kentucky, was active in the work of the group, although his order did not allow him to be a board member.[141]

Since the Committee was not a membership organization, these men were technically board members. To be a board member, however, was to be a "worker" in "a network of people around the South." Their main task was to look for crisis situations, such as an execution or a racial conflict. In such an event, several of the members would travel to the site to investigate.[142]

After several years, Campbell chose to disband the organization, beginning with removing himself as publisher of *Katallagete*.

---

[139]Second interview by author.

[140]Campbell and James Y. Holloway, *Up to Our Steeples in Politics* (New York: Paulist Press, 1970), 1-3. Campbell and Holloway collaborated on several books and articles when they worked together with the Committee of Southern Churchmen.

[141]Ibid. The names given in this interview were representative, not exhaustive. For a detailed description of the membership of the Committee of Southern Churchmen, see Robin Jimmerson, "A Sociological Analysis of the Prophetic Ministry of Will D. Campbell" (Ph.D. diss., Southern Baptist Theological Seminary, 1990).

[142]Ibid.

He removed himself from the organization in an effort to live consistently with his distrust of institutions. Campbell accepted the need for organizations, but he saw it as a limited need. Most organizations start out of good motives and regress into self-centeredness as they age. He hoped to avoid that development with the Committee.

> [W]hen I was working for this here thing we called the Committee of Southern Churchmen there was enough dissatisfaction among young people, and some not so young, in the South, and I was going to enough places to speak . . . [to] people who were committed to the same things I was committed to . . . that I could have started another movement.[143]

Campbell had no doubt that he could have recruited a large number of people for the new organization, but to do so would have been a contradiction in his values. "[I]f I say I don't trust institutions," Campbell commented, "and then go out and start one, that's going to negate what I just said."[144] Educated and shaped by his work within three traditional institutional ministries, Campbell made a great effort to live consistently with his religious world view.

Conclusion

Will D. Campbell's journey from Amite County, Mississippi, to Nashville, Tennessee, covered a great distance in more ways than just geographical. By the time Campbell left the National Council of Churches, he had worked for three institutional ministries, leaving each one disillusioned. His final exit not only disillusioned him; it also forced him to reassess the validity of all structures. Campbell's experience impressed on him the view that

---

[143] Second interview by author.
[144] Ibid.

sin has corporate dimensions, a view that was reinforced by the theology of Karl Barth and Jacques Ellul.

From the time he left home for Louisiana College, Campbell was in a state of development. Upon his departure from the NCC, the development was complete. Campbell believed in a religiously-motivated, Christocentric approach to social issues. He also hoped to address social problems from an anti-institutional, individual perspective. The formation of the Committee of Southern Churchmen was not only a means to support him after he left the NCC. It was also an attempt to put into practice his new understanding of social action without utopian motives and without undue concern for the needs of the organization. The disbanding of the organization, then, was not a sign of failure, but one of success.

Since 1963 when he left the NCC, Campbell's social and religious thought has remained basically unchanged. The remainder of his work, whether as social activist, author, or renegade minister, was shaped by the lessons he appropriated from these formative years. Campbell's actions since 1963 have embodied two salient characteristics. First, he has continued to display a strong social consciousness motivated by an explicitly religious world view. Second, he has tried to live consistently with his world view, especially his distrust of institutions.

Chapter 2

Out From Under the Steeples:
Campbell's Ethics and Theology

Campbell's departure from the National Council of Churches and the formation of the Committee of Southern Churchmen marked more than a transition in his employment. Campbell's vocation, however, was not the only thing that he reevaluated. His experiences forced him also to examine the shape of his theology and ethical thought. What did he now believe as a result of his experiences in the parish, academy, and interdenominational bureaucracy?

The 1960s marked a turning point in Campbell's thinking. The social activist began to question some of his earlier utopian notions. The Committee of Southern Churchmen, while providing him a forum to address selected issues, did not see itself in the business of building a new society, and neither did Campbell. Campbell now wanted to express his thought in more explicitly religious terms. While he continued as a social activist, Campbell wanted to speak in the language of faith, with a special emphasis on portions of the writings of Paul and the ethical teachings of Jesus. Campbell's affinity with these two strains in biblical literature resulted from a desire to express Christian faith in terms other than those established by contemporary theology. At this time Campbell also revised his approach to the race question. He came to believe that many of the clergy and church agencies in the civil rights movement had acted out of humanitarian, rather than theological, motivations. Campbell preferred for the churches to speak to the race issue as the Church speaking in the language of the Church.

This chapter will investigate the ethics and theology of Campbell. First, the chapter will discuss a third and final conversion moment for Campbell when he radically altered his approach to the race issue. This experience—his response to the death of a civil rights worker—motivated Campbell to a new understanding of the source of racial animosity. Campbell increasingly saw racism as more than a legal problem. Racism stemmed from the nature of humanity, and human nature was beyond the reach of government.

Campbell believed that only the Church could address the role of human nature in racism. The degree to which the Church would answer was another matter. Since so many elements in the institutional church did not support civil rights, and since so many elements outside the institutional church did, one must question Campbell's strong endorsement of the Church's potential. To a significant degree, government had a greater influence on human nature than the Church.

Second, this chapter will discuss the theological elements in Campbell's thought. Influenced by Jacques Ellul and Vernard Eller, Campbell has described himself as a "Christian Anarchist." The chapter will discuss Campbell's understanding of Christian anarchy and how it has changed Campbell's understanding of political solutions to human problems. In addition, the chapter discusses the role of neo-orthodoxy in Campbell's theology, highlighting a number of key neo-orthodox ideas. Among these are his emphasis on divine sovereignty, human finitude, corporate sin, and the need for the religious community to speak the language of faith and revelation. His theology, however, did not create his social ethic. Instead, Campbell's already-developed social ethic led him to Neo-Orthodox theology. For Campbell, ethics precedes theology.

A New Perspective on Race Relations and Social Activism

Seeking an approach more specifically grounded in his understanding of Christianity, Campbell began to change his approach to social issues during the 1960s. His speech to the Conference on Religion and Race in 1963 was one of the first public expressions of his call for a stronger theological motivation for social activism.[1] Campbell had come to believe that many religious social activists were motivated by concerns other than noble humanitarianism.

Race relations was the most popular social concern among liberal whites and, to put it in his typically blunt style, Campbell believed many white social activists joined the civil rights movement because it was a trend. A number of problems resulted from this perspective. First, social activists viewed the race issue in utopian terms, thinking that a successful push for civil rights would create the millennium. Second, the popularity of the issue meant that many social activists, Campbell included, were motivated not only by social justice, but by a desire to be on the right side of the issue. In other words, utilitarian concerns played a role in many people's participation in the civil rights movement.

Moreover, Campbell held that integration was being equated with the Christian religion, rather than being seen as an implication of the Christian religion. Campbell also determined that he was as guilty as anyone in making this connection. He had traded the moralistic code of fundamentalism for another moralism. A graphic conversation with his brother, described in *Brother to a Dragonfly*, helped Campbell come to this realization. Campbell's brother, Joe, had been institutionalized in the 1960s for drug addiction, and Campbell traveled to visit him. Although Joe had introduced Will to many socially progressive ideas and thinkers, including Howard Fast, Joe's language by this time reflected old racist habits. Language notwithstanding, Campbell's brother made a point: white social liberals, including Will Campbell, participated in the civil rights movement as much to help themselves as to express the Christian religion. Joe Campbell said,

> Maybe you're the one who needs help. You think you're going to save the . . . South with integration, with putting niggers in every schoolhouse and on every five-and-dime

---

[1]*Brother to a Dragonfly*, 229-232.

store lunch counter stool, and locking them up in the same
nut hatch with white folks. . . . What you're saying is that
you're going to use the niggers to save yourself. What's so
Christian about that? . . . Your niggers are like my pills.
They prop you liberals up and make you feel good. . . .[2]

Along with other factors, this comment from his brother caused
Campbell to reassess his role as a social activist. Rather than
changing his concern for social justice, Campbell changed his
perspective on social problems. He began to think of himself less
as a social activist and more as a Christian with a social conscience.
Such a reorientation primarily had to do with Campbell's starting
place for social action. Does social activism inform the Christian
faith, or does the Christian faith inform one's social activism.
Social activism had been the starting point for Campbell, but he
was moving to a more specifically religious orientation. Thus, his
move out of institutional ministry was not merely a matter of
burnout. Campbell was not disillusioned with the Christian faith
as much as he was disillusioned with certain approaches to faith.

No single event can be credited with Campbell's renewed
insistence upon a specifically Christian worldview. The change
must be seen as a long process, in many ways beginning with his
theological education at Yale and extending through his attempts
to apply that education in various ministries. Certain events,
however, stand out as catalysts for Campbell's insights. His
relationship with two very different men—P. D. East and Jonathan
Daniels—provided such moments.

Born in 1921 in Columbia, Mississippi, P. D. East was the son
of a mentally ill woman who placed him up for immediate
adoption. His adoptive father was a laborer in the timber industry
in south Mississippi, which required the family to move often from
one town to another. After a lonely childhood, East graduated
from high school, attended a junior college for a short time, and
eventually ended up in Hattiesburg as an employee of a railroad

---

[2]Ibid., 201.

company.[3] An independent man who often challenged authority, East did not relish the status of being an employee. Seeking more control over his job situation, East became the first editor of the *Union Review*, a newspaper for the Coke and Chemical Workers Union. East did not work with the paper because he sympathized with the Union movement. He edited the *Union Review* for two reasons: the freedom it provided and the income it generated, two-thirds of which went to East himself.[4]

Eventually, East started another paper for the Garment Workers' Union, the *Local Advocate*. East had greater control over this second paper, and he kept ninety percent of the profits. The college drop-out and social rebel had entered the mainstream of society. In 1953, he acquired a third paper, *The Petal Paper*, published in rural Forest County. At first, this paper was a traditional, small-town weekly, designed to inform the community and to bring a profit to the owner. After the Supreme Court ruled in 1954 that segregation was unconstitutional, however, East used the paper as a forum to lampoon the political leadership of the state in their efforts to resist integration.[5]

Campbell first came into contact with East while working at the University of Mississippi. They gravitated to each other because of their mutual challenges to the state's segregation policies.[6] Before East became acquainted with Campbell personally, he heard about Campbell's actions surrounding Religious Emphasis Week. East admired Campbell for refusing to withdraw the invitation to Alvin Kershaw, despite pressure from the university's administration. "I was not acquainted with the Reverend Mr. Campbell," East recalled in his autobiography, "but I began to feel a mounting respect for at least one minister in the state."[7]

---

[3]P. D. East, *The Magnolia Jungle: The Life, Times, and Education of a Southern Editor* (New York: Simon and Schuster, 1960), ix, 16-19, 93-98.

[4]Ibid., 112.

[5]Ibid., 113, 125-128, 133.

[6]*Brother to a Dragonfly*, 216.

[7]East, 158.

Before long, the two men did become personally acquainted and began helping each other in their respective involvement in the state's racial crisis. In 1956 East worked with William Faulkner to publish a single-edition satire on segregation, *The Southern Reposure*. Faulkner did not write for the paper, but he promised to offer his advice and financial assistance. East wrote an editorial and gathered some articles, but all articles were listed anonymously. In his editorial, East used the fictitious name, Nathan Bedford Cooclose. Hoping to rally racial moderates in the state, East felt his best opportunities lay in targeting Mississippi universities. Campbell agreed to help distribute East's paper on the campus of the University of Mississippi.[8]

Campbell also encouraged East to continue publication of *The Petal Paper* when adversaries began attacking it for its stance on the race issue. When the newspaper began challenging the state's resistance to the Supreme Court's desegregation ruling of 1954, it quickly lost local support. However, the weekly secured sympathetic readers in other regions of the country. Following the advice of many, including Campbell, East continued publication. "Even the Yankees," Campbell told East, "[will] think there is still some hope for us as long as your paper keeps going."[9]

East and Campbell often discussed religion, with Campbell attempting "to set him straight on one theological point or another." In one significant conversation, East challenged the validity of Christianity because of failures he perceived in the institutional church. Campbell agreed with East's assessment of institutional religion. The record of the institution, however, "didn't have anything to do with the Christian Faith."

Campbell thus separated institutional religion from his understanding of authentic Christianity. Since to Campbell Christianity and the institutional church were two different things, East asked Campbell to define the Christian faith—in twenty-five words or less. Campbell answered with his classic, iconoclastic

---

[8]Ibid., 194-196, 294.
[9]Ibid., 240.

definition of Christianity: "We're all bastards, but God loves us anyway."[10] Christianity, for Campbell, had its basic meaning in the universal love of God for humanity. The concise, earthy statement impressed East both with the definition and with Campbell himself. "It made sense to me, but I didn't rejoin the church. There aren't enough Wills to go around," East wrote in his 1960 autobiography.[11] Five years later, an event provided East an opportunity to test Campbell's definition of Christianity, a test that would become another "conversion" for Campbell's religious thought.[12]

East became a personal friend with Campbell's brother, Joe, each helping the other in a time of need. The first need belonged to East. His provocative editorials brought death threats against him and his family, forcing him in 1964 to relocate to Fairhope, Alabama, about forty miles south of Mobile. From his new location in Fairhope, East continued to publish his paper, which by this time existed primarily to challenge legal segregation rather than as a community weekly. Despite living outside the state, East still had to return to Mississippi for various reasons, although at great risk to his safety. On these trips, Joe hid East in his pharmacy and helped him slip across the state line without detection. Joe eventually needed the help of a friend when he was suffering from chemical dependency and facing marital problems. Knowing the problems of his troubled friend, East invited Joe to move into his home in Fairhope, Alabama.[13]

Shortly after moving Joe to Fairhope, East sensed that Joe's problems were more severe than he had realized, and he asked Will to drive down from Nashville. Meanwhile, events elsewhere in Alabama provided East the backdrop to challenge Campbell's

---

[10]*Brother to a Dragonfly*, 220-221.

[11]East, 206.

[12]*Brother to a Dragonfly*, 221-227.

[13]Ibid., 216. *The Petal Paper* was published weekly from 1953 until 1960. From 1960 until 1972, the paper was published both monthly and bimonthly. See First Search, 4178093.

penetrating definition of Christianity. Just north of Fairhope, in Lowndes County, Alabama, a temporary deputy sheriff named Tom Coleman shot and killed Jonathan Daniels, a civil rights activist.

Daniels was a student at the Episcopal Theological Seminary in Massachusetts. Like many socially active seminarians of his time, he became involved in the civil rights movement and traveled to Lowndes County in 1965 to help register African Americans to vote.[14] In August, his involvement in a protest march resulted in his arrest and imprisonment for several days in the county jail. Hours after his release on August 20, Daniels joined Richard Morrisoe, Ruby Sales, and Joyce Bailey several miles outside of town. The group proceeded to the Cash Store, a small country grocery store where blacks frequently shopped. As Daniels and Sales attempted to enter the store, Coleman shot Daniels at point blank range with a shotgun, killing him instantly.[15]

When Campbell arrived at East's home, the news of Daniels's death had just broken. Campbell had met Daniels a few weeks earlier when the two attended an annual meeting of the Southern Christian Leadership Conference in Birmingham and was impressed with the depth of Daniels's commitment. Daniels' death now provided East the opportunity to test the definition of Christianity that Campbell had given several years earlier. East and Campbell began their discussion:

---

[14]Charles W. Eagles, *Outside Agitator: Jon Daniels and the Civil Rights Movement in Alabama* (Chapel Hill: The University of North Carolina Press, 1993), 119.

[15]Ibid., 171, 178-179. Coleman was not charged with first degree murder, but with first degree manslaughter for the death of Daniels and assault and battery for the wounding of Morrisoe. The trial began on Monday, September 27, 1965 and ended on the following Thursday morning when the jury returned a verdict of not guilty. In 1991, the Episcopal Church named Daniels as a martyr on its Calendar of Lesser Feasts and Fasts. Ibid., 202, 206, 243, 264. See also Jonathan Myrick Daniels, *The Jon Daniels Story, with his Letters and Papers*, ed. William J. Schneider (New York: Seabury Press, 1967); and William J. Schneider, *American Martyr: The Jon Daniels Story* (Milwaukee: Morehouse Publishing, 1992).

Was Jonathan a bastard? . . . I knew that if I said no he would leave me alone and if I said yes he wouldn't. And I knew my definition would be blown if I said no. So I said, 'Yes.' All right. Is Thomas Coleman a bastard? That one was a lot easier. Yes, Thomas Coleman is a bastard. [East replied] Okay. Let me get this straight. . . . Jonathan Daniels *was* a bastard. Thomas Coleman *is* a bastard. . . . Which one of these two bastards do you think God loves the most?[16]

This emotional conversation was a "conversion" for Campbell. He came to feel that he had based his involvement in social activism on political and humanitarian motivations, not on a Christian worldview. Campbell felt that all his actions of the past twenty years had been "a ministry of liberal sophistication" that based its ethics on Supreme Court rulings, Enlightenment thought, and "a theology of law and order."[17] Campbell realized that the starting place for his actions had been political and religious liberalism.

I had never considered myself a liberal. I didn't think in those terms. But that was the camp in which I had pitched my tent. Now I was not so sure. . . . Conversion is at once a joyous and painful experience. If it was not the beginning of my ministry it was certainly a turning point. And it was certainly the most significant theological training I had received since we sat at our father's fireside and listened to him read the Bible every night.

What was this conversion? It was not so much a change in what Campbell did or believed as it was a change in his perspective or approach. Campbell believed that in his prior approach to social activism he had been more concerned to be "a doctrinaire social

---

[16]*Brother to a Dragonfly*, 221.
[17]Ibid., 222.

activist" than a Christian minister.[18] Campbell's new understanding of Christianity meant that he must reject the "law" of social activism for the "grace" of the Christian message. The particular type of Christian grace to which Campbell now adhered was Pauline, based especially on Paul's writings in Corinthians. The Christian social activist should not be governed by laws, but should act out of "an ethos, a condition of being, *In Christ*."[19]

From this time forward, Campbell decided that the role of the Christian in race relations differed from that of other activists. The Christian must now act as if race is irrelevant. The concept of God reconciling the world, discussed in 2 Corinthians 5:15, became his basic text. For Campbell, this text meant that classifying humans according to racial categories was decidedly un-Christian. The Christian message, for Campbell, involved more than making African Americans and whites equal in legal terms. It meant making the question of race irrelevant. Jonathan Daniels embodied this notion by dying as an ordained white minister working for racial integration.[20]

As Campbell reflected on his own work in the civil rights movement, he felt that his approach to the dispossessors did not reflect a proper Christian orientation. He had "learned to cuss Mississippi and Alabama sheriffs, [and] learned to say 'redneck' with the same venomous tones we had heard others, or ourselves, say 'nigger.'"[21] A Christian worldview, according to Campbell, must "never take sides." Christian social action must not only be interested in those who are mistreated; it must also be interested in changing those who do the mistreating.

> We were right in aligning ourselves with the black sufferer. But we were wrong in not directing some of our patience

---

[18]Ibid., 222, 225.

[19]Ibid., 227.

[20]*Race and the Renewal of the Church* (Philadelphia: Westminster Press, 1962), 9-10.

[21]*Brother to a Dragonfly*, 226.

and energy and action to a group which also had a history [the poor whites].[22]

Although many influences caused Campbell to change his approach to social action and race relations, he pointed to the encounter with East as a decisive moment. It was for Campbell a discovery of an expressly Christian approach to social action. From that moment, Campbell was comfortable seeing himself first and foremost in religious terms.

While East impressed Campbell, Campbell impressed East as well. East recorded in his autobiography that he wanted Will Campbell to be among the ministers officiating at his funeral. When East died, about ten years after he wrote his book, Campbell was the only one of the ministers he had mentioned still living. He conducted the funeral via "a telephone conference call."[23] Campbell later commented that this was a fitting memorial "for a man who took delight in being a pagan, befriended my brother when no one else would, and led me to the Lord."[24]

The conversion that grew out of the encounter with P. D. East changed Campbell's outlook. While many of Campbell's actions and concerns remained the same—he was still an advocate of racial integration—his perspectives were different. Campbell believed that his approach to social issues had now become expressly Christian. Moreover, his concern became less a matter of building a more just society and more a matter of seeing that the Church respond in a way that was consistent with its ethics. In other words, the Church's concern in the area of civil rights was no longer a matter of merely ending discrimination for a dispossessed community. Christian race relations was about reconciling ethnic groups into a community and making these groups aware of their status before God, as Campbell understood that concept.

---

[22]Ibid.
[23]East, 242; *Brother to a Dragonfly*, 228.
[24]*Brother to a Dragonfly*, 228.

While the larger civil rights movement was concerned with behavior, Campbell said that the Christian approach to race relations must be concerned with the feelings and attitudes of all involved. In *Forty Acres and a Goat*, Campbell wrote of a conversation he had with an activist involved in desegregating restaurants. The protester said, "I don't give a damn if I make them sick. I don't care if they vomit in their plate when I'm eating in that restaurant. Just so they don't try to stop me from being there."

This approach, which was concerned only with securing one's legal right to eat in a public facility, fell short of a comprehensive Christian approach. The Christian approach, informed by the concept of reconciliation, must speak not only to securing the right to be present in the restaurant. This approach must speak to the relationship of all present, Campbell believed, "for surely we are created to love one another." Securing legal rights is not sufficient. "It has to be alright that the other is there," Campbell said, "or old attitudes will . . . recapitulate old behavior."[25]

Campbell, then, changed his approach to social activism while remaining a social activist. This new approach, however, caused him to expand his range of interests and actions. Reconciliation among the races entailed more than concern only with the African American community. Out of a desire to act first as a person of faith rather than as a political activist, Campbell reached out to the white community to change its attitudes, especially the attitudes of the poor whites from whose ranks the Ku Klux Klan often drew its members.

Campbell could be concerned with the white and the African American communities now because of his new insight into a Christian worldview. The church should no longer think in terms of race, but of building a common humanity. In the early church, Campbell argued, "race was irrelevant." The solution to race relations was building a community where people laid aside racial considerations. Even the dispossessed community must begin to think in terms that transcend race. From a distinctively Christian

---

[25]*Forty Acres and a Goat*, 270.

point of view, a person must think in terms of a common humanity. "The Christian," Campbell wrote in his first book, *Race and the Renewal of the Church*, "does not speak as a white man, a Negro, an Oriental, or an Occidental." Too many in the Christian community, however, had been speaking and acting in those very terms, as well as terms informed by the latest social and political trends.

The Christian approach to racial and social problems, according to Campbell, should also transcend any human ideology. Prevailing ideologies, according to Campbell, had motivated most of the religious community's social activism, making them highly selective in their issues of concern. This concern to act out of non-ideological conciliatory motivations, however, drew Campbell to reach out to the white community. Moreover, this idea of reconciliation was not simply a pragmatic means of winning the loyalty of racists to the cause of desegregation. This approach is concerned with showing compassion and giving aid to people even if those same people do not accept one's cause.

This new perspective, then, allowed Campbell to reach out to segregationists while at the same time supporting the work of civil rights activists. Campbell lamented that the religious community had neglected this element. The segregationist, however, "is a child of God. He too is a brother."[26] In Campbell's understanding of the Pauline idea of reconciliation, black and white were already reconciled in God's eyes. The segregationist, of course, lived a denial of that reconciliation. The integrationist, however, also lived a denial when failing to accept the common humanity of these dispossessors. Too many people in the civil rights movement, Campbell wrote, including himself in the allegation, thought of segregationists as the enemy to be defeated. The Christian approach, however, must see the "tragedy" of the segregationist." "One who understands the nature of tragedy can never take sides. And I," Campbell admitted, "had taken sides."[27]

---

[26]*Race and the Renewal of the Church*, 8, 23.
[27]*Brother to a Dragonfly*, 226.

Before addressing social integration, the Christian social activist should "first of all be concerned with souls." This concern distinguishes Christian social activism from humanitarian or secular social activism. Campbell did not reject the approach of secularism. He saw that approach, however, as having a different concern from Christian reconciliation. When a social activist is concerned with souls—with one's status before God—that person's "anguish as the suffering of the victims of racism will not blind him to the dangers facing the souls of the oppressors."[28] From Campbell's new Christian perspective, "Christ's death and resurrection is for Eldridge Cleaver [a Black Panther leader] and Robert Shelton, the Imperial Wizard of the Ku Klux Klan."[29]

Shortly after Campbell came to his new awareness of the implications of Christian reconciliation, he began reaching out to members of the Ku Klux Klan. Formed in the years after the Civil War, the Ku Klux Klan was a terrorist organization designed to prevent the former slaves from gaining political power. This original Klan, which had many members from the southern aristocracy, eventually faded away, only to be revived in the 1920s. The new Klan was a much stronger organization, with more members, including many community leaders. This second wave of Klan activity also subsided, only to be renewed during the rise of the civil rights movement. This latest resurgence of the Klan, however, though perhaps more violent than earlier Klan organizations, did not draw members from the upper echelon of society. The new Klan most often drew its members from the poorest in the white community. They were often victims themselves of poverty, which they mistakenly blamed on the African American community.[30] It was also a mistake, however, to blame the Klan for causing racism. The Klan's violence, Campbell argued, was not the

---

[28]*Race and the Renewal of the Church*, 42.

[29]"Prophet, Poet, Preacher-at-Large: A Conversation with Will Campbell," interview by Norman Bowman, *The Student*, December 1970, 30.

[30]David Mark Chalmers, *Hooded Americanism: the History of the Ku Klux Klan* (New York: New Viewpoints, 1981), passim.

source of racism, but rather a symptom. These people were bound by a "cycle of milltown squalor, [and] generations of poverty." The source of racism was in the economic structure of the country, and "a pitiful and powerless few people marching around a burning cross in a Carolina cow pasture" did not control these structures.[31]

Campbell had trouble at first reaching out to these poor whites because of the violence associated with them. He affirmed the idea of racial reconciliation, but his natural instinct was to do so with a condition. He would have all people reconciled with God and one another "unless they murder civil rights workers in Mississippi or club demonstrators in Alabama." Reconciliation as God's universal acceptance of all people is what Campbell calls the "scandal" of the Christian message. Campbell confessed his natural reaction is: "I don't like it. I want somebody to be left out. I want somebody to be beyond the pale." Campbell knew that reaction, however, to be an emotional reaction not rooted in his understanding of the theological implications of Christianity.[32]

Because Campbell believed it important to translate his belief in human reconciliation into action, he took measures to reach out to people in the Ku Klux Klan. He did not make contact with these people simply because they were in the Klan. As Campbell understood his actions, he made contact with Klansmen in spite of their membership in the Klan. "I never did pal with anybody because he was in the Klan. But I never did ask anybody to get out." He saw them as troubled people in need of the services of the ministry.

Campbell's concern for these people stemmed from Campbell's very literal reading of Luke 4: 16-21. This New Testament passage describes Jesus reading a selection from Isaiah, which describes the speaker as having come "to bring good news to the poor" and "to proclaim release to the captives." Campbell has attempted to read this passage without an ideological bias, seeing it as applicable to

---

[31]*Brother to a Dragonfly*, 245.
[32]Chapel Address at Southern Baptist Theological Seminary, Louisville, Kentucky, 9 March 1983, Sound Recording.

unpopular groups. His understanding of Christianity allowed him to reach out to Klansmen because he found "nothing in the Scripture about ideology, nothing about political views, . . . [nothing that said] visit the sick if they are morally sound." As Campbell got to know some of these people, he visited them in jail and in the hospital. He also performed marriages and funerals for them, because he saw them as people in need. Although Campbell's actions seemed at first contrary to the civil rights movement, they were actually an attempt to apply a Christian view of charity to all persons. He noted:

> The passage from Isaiah that Jesus used as his inaugural address statement [contains] . . . nothing about ideology. It talks about prisoners, [but] there's no condition set.

Campbell also saw his response to white racists not only as a ministry to their needs but also as a more effective way to address the causes of racism. "If you are interested in trying to improve the relationship between the races," Campbell explained, "then you go where the problem is. . . . The root of the problem was in the white community."[33] The basic problem, Campbell thought, was religious in nature, not political. Because the religious community failed to address the race problem from a sufficiently religious worldview, it failed to be concerned with the problems of the poor whites. From a Christian perspective, racial problems could not be solved without a concern for all the parties involved.

The enlightened whites of the South, Campbell proposed, acted with great pride in rejecting any concern for poor whites. In their attempt to fight racism, white church leaders committed to integration vented as much anger toward racists as they did toward racism. This approach stemmed from eagerness on the part of enlightened whites to overcompensate for the racist views of other whites of the South. To prove non-prejudice, whites often went out of their way to demonstrate antipathy toward racists as people.

---

[33]Second interview by author.

Campbell warned against this attitude, reminding the white social activists, including himself, to "ask ourselves what happened in our lives to make us so different from the racist." He added: "Somehow we cannot hate the racist, for most of us do not know how or when we left his ranks, if we have left them at all."[34]

White civil rights activists, in leaving the ranks of the racists, often developed a sense of social elitism, Campbell believed. While this attitude may or may not have been conscious, it was nonetheless real. Moreover, social elitism was itself a form of racism, and Campbell admitted that he played a part in this type of racist approach. For example, one of Campbell's first assignments with the NCC was to counter the work of a Nashville Klan activist, John Kasper. Kasper had moved to Tennessee specifically to organize violent opposition to integration. White civil rights activists took efforts to discredit not only Kasper's work, but Kasper himself. It was not so much the effort to oppose Kasper that Campbell later lamented as it was the approach. Kasper was to be exposed as a fraud and an opportunist who had a black girlfriend, a fact that would have eliminated his support among his racist audience. "The efforts of the liberals to discredit Kasper," Campbell claimed, "were as racist as his advocates." In retrospect, Campbell felt that circulating photographs of Kasper dancing with his "black girlfriend" took advantage of mores against interracial social relations, rather than challenging them.[35]

Campbell also challenged the traditional approach of civil rights activists when he spoke at a conference on the Klan and violence. His speech followed a film produced by CBS, entitled, "The Ku Klux Klan: An Invisible Empire." Watching the film reinforced Campbell's awareness that social activism had neglected its responsibility to the poor whites. When he rose to introduce himself, Campbell said, "My name is Will Campbell. I'm a Baptist preacher. I'm a native of Mississippi. And I'm pro-Klansman because I'm pro-human being."

---

[34]*Race and the Renewal of the Church*, 24-25.
[35]*Forty Acres and a Goat*, 50.

The self-introduction enraged the audience, and many stormed away from the meeting. Those who remained became, in Campbell's view, "everything they thought the Ku Klux Klan to be—hostile, frustrated, angry, violent and irrational." The reaction demonstrated Campbell's belief that social activism had become captive to an ideology that contradicted his Christian understanding of reconciliation. For Campbell, reconciliation meant that one could embrace a member of the Ku Klux Klan as a human without endorsing the ideology of the Klan. To reject a person's humanity because of his or her ideology is itself a rigidly ideological view, according to Campbell. He later commented:

> I never was able to explain to them that pro-Klans*man* is not the same as pro-Klan. That the former has to do with a person, the other with an ideology. I tried to stand patiently, even in the face of fear and danger, because I had so recently learned that lesson myself.

The audience's reaction provided a good example of Campbell's belief in the failed perspective of social activism without a strong grounding in his understanding of Christianity. By ridiculing the poor white racists, the audience both neglected a victimized group and failed to address the structural sources of racism. Poor whites, even Klansmen, did not control the sources of power in society. Society was controlled, according to Campbell, not by the lower classes, but by the upper classes and their institutions. Those who actually control society are the ones who should be held accountable for social ills, especially racism. A particular irony existed, Campbell observed, in the fact that the audience was composed of people who came from privileged backgrounds. There was also irony in that the film was "produced for their edification and enjoyment by the Establishment of the establishment—CBS"

> I sensed that there wasn't a radical in the bunch. For if they were radical how could they laugh at a poor ignorant farmer who didn't know his left hand from his right. If they

had been radical they would have been weeping, asking what had produced him.[36]

Campbell did not attempt to write a systematic theology of Christian reconciliation and social problems, but he did describe how the reconciliation based on Pauline ideas in II Corinthians would change one's approach to social problems. People in the Church, according to Campbell, should respond instinctively to social ills. That is, a Christian should not take a position on an issue because it is a liberal or conservative position. A Christian should, on impulse, respond without regard to large social and political issues. "A Christian," Campbell said, "is someone who doesn't think [about how to respond]. . . . By that, I meant that it's instinct." Campbell's understanding of the Christian doctrine of man as informed by the writings of Paul eliminates the need for the practicing Christian to rely heavily on any particular social or political view. This rejection of ideology is part of what Campbell meant by responding instinctively:

> Paul said when one is in Christ . . . a person is a new creature. . . . I know the psychologists are saying that the human beings don't have instincts, but that's not what Paul was saying. We instinctively [if a person is a Christian] know what's just and decent and honorable and right.[37]

Up to Our Steeples in Politics, one of Campbell's early books, expressed many of his sentiments about reconciliation as a distinctively Christian approach to social problems and human relations. Despite the good intentions of so many socially progressive church activists, Campbell concluded that this group had exchanged the rigid requirements of fundamentalism for the rigid requirements of social activism. Good people supported certain

---

[36]*Brother to a Dragonfly*, 243-244.
[37]Second interview by author.

causes, and bad people opposed certain causes. Support for a cause often translated into support for a political position, and it is that approach that Campbell thought violated the intent of Christian reconciliation. Instead of political solutions, the Christian approach entails "life as a thanksgiving to God. . . . [I]n other words, life as the Good News . . . not social action."[38] Based on an understanding of the New Testament, this approach claimed, "something has been done for" humanity; namely, the restoration of all people to a common humanity and a new human nature through the work of Jesus.[39] The institutional churches, however, "have failed in . . . their ministry because (at their liberal best) they sought to do for the world [through political solutions] what God has already done for the world in Christ."[40]

This approach was hardly instinctive or reflective of a new human nature, especially when set against Campbell's embrace of certain elements of the teachings of Paul and Jesus. Campbell wanted the church to be socially active, but he wanted this activism to flow naturally. He did not want socially responsible Christians to withdraw from activism, but he wanted them to "dispense with the scorecards."[41] Campbell believed that the Christian message essentially meant that God embraced all persons unconditionally. One should not engage in social activism to win God's approval; one should engage in it because of an awareness of one's status with God.

> I don't object to the doing as much as I object to the scorecard, the talking about it [social action], the imprison-

---

[38]Campbell and James Y. Holloway, *Up to Our Steeples in Politics* (New York: Paulist Press, 1970), 3-4.

[39]"What Do We Do About What Has Been Done?" Address to the 51st Annual Ministers Week at Emory University, Atlanta, 1 January 1986, Sound Recording.

[40]*Up to Our Steeples in Politics*, 1-2.

[41]"What Do We Do About What Has Been Done?"

ing of it by institutionalizing it and saying, "This is the Way."[42]

Campbell's claim that this universal acceptance of humans by God represents the message of the Bible is something of an overstatement. In reality, scripture gives multiple perspectives on God's view of humanity. In some texts, humans seem reconciled to God, and in others humanity is estranged from God. While Campbell's stress on God's universal acceptance of humanity is the most positive image of God presented in the Bible, it is not the only one. Campbell has in fact selected one particular image from the many contradictory images in scripture.

Campbell, then, applies his anti-institutional worldview even to ethical systems. This attitude, however, while growing out of Campbell's experience, does not reflect cynicism or nihilism. While a quick reading of some of Campbell's statements on social issues may appear to present a disillusioned religious social activist, Campbell rejected comprehensive ethical systems as a means of being faithful to Christianity as he understood it. The ethical systems soon become self-perpetuating structures with their own agendas, he argued. When people act instinctively, they do not need an ethical system to guide them. They will automatically know to do the right thing.

Comprehensive ethical approaches, according to Campbell, become systems that create their own agendas, soon replacing the idea of an instinctive approach. "There is an implied 'oughtness' in the system of ethics," Campbell said.[43] This "oughtness" prevents a holistic, Christian response by forcing people into particular ideological camps. For example, a conservative might support the death penalty and oppose abortion, while a liberal might support abortion and oppose nuclear weapons. For Campbell, these divided concerns result from a person approaching an issue first as a conservative or liberal rather than as a Christian. If

---

[42]Dibble interview, 172.
[43]Ibid., 171.

a Christian holds to the sacredness of life, then liberalism or conservatism becomes irrelevant. Campbell argues:

> Life to me is its own meaning, it's sacred. That's why I oppose the destruction of human life in any form, whether it's by the death penalty or whether it's by aborting unborn babies . . . or whether it's by nuclear holocaust. I don't. . . begin to comprehend how anybody can have one of those concerns and not have all of them.[44]

Campbell would not force even this position upon another person, however. A person must not oppose abortion and the death penalty in order to be a Christian, for this position would be reverting to the legalism that Campbell opposed. Campbell thinks that a Christian's ideas and actions should flow naturally or instinctively. He recognized that modern psychiatry and psychology reject the idea of instincts, but he simply rejects their conclusions.[45]

A Christian is not a Christian by virtue of holding a certain position. That is, Campbell no longer equates authentic Christianity with support for desegregation, nor would he say that one must oppose the death penalty to win the approval of God. The position will grow out of one's Christianity, which Campbell called discipleship.

> Discipleship is the struggle to be like Christ, even though I know I am not Christ and that I am not going to be like Christ perfectly. But I am expected to try. Once I make what I *believe* the issue, then I'm off the hook. I either believe your particular creed [whether the "creed" is liberalism or fundamentalism] or I don't.[46]

---

[44]Ibid., 162.

[45]Second interview by author.

[46]"Interview with Will Campbell," interview by Bill McNabb, *The Door*, March/April 1990, 12-15.

Yet, discipleship thus explained is problematic. While one does not do certain actions to become a practicing Christian, it certainly seems that the practicing person of faith will feel compelled to engage in certain behaviors and actions.

Campbell's new approach to social issues, then, is an attempt on his part to move away from political activism and toward a Christian orientation to the world. He became disillusioned with institutions, but not with the Christian message as he understood it. Concerned that the Christian community had lost its distinctive voice by adopting the prevailing social and political agendas, Campbell recast his thought in the Pauline language of reconciliation. He believed that the Pauline interpretation of the work of Christ meant that all humans had been reconciled to one another. For Campbell, the concept of reconciliation is the fundamental message of the New Testament. The duty of the Church was to embody that reconciliation, not to create it. Finally, he believed that reconciliation results when the Church acts instinctively in its social activism. The Christian message is that "the hatred, warfare, and death between and among us is over: God is with us the way He is with us in Jesus."[47]

These words can appear to be semantic games. On the one hand, Campbell presents a positive image of the divine by proclaiming an understanding of a God who accepts all people and asks that humans reflect that acceptance in their relationships. However, the distinction between instinctive acts and non-instinctive acts is a difficult argument to make. How can one know if a deed of charity is being done in response to God's love or to earn God's love? It seems that the two motivations are symbiotic.

Campbell and Christian Anarchy

---

[47]Campbell and Holloway,". . . *and the criminals with him*. . ." (New York: Paulist Press, 1973), 141-142.

Campbell's renewed sense of Christian orientation grew out of his positive and negative experiences as a social activist, culminating in his response to the death of Jonathan Daniels. Because of this new Christian orientation, Campbell has hesitated to identify himself with any political movement or theological trend in an effort to transcend ideology.

This attempt to move beyond ideology is not the approach of Campbell alone. Thinkers Vernard Eller and Jacques Ellul have taken a similar approach, calling it Christian anarchy. This current theological phrase, moreover, has been the one phrase that Campbell willingly embraced because Christian anarchy is largely an attempt to transcend the traditional right/left dichotomy. Stating that his actions since the 1960s have not been "political acts . . . categorized by someone's scheme as 'Left' or 'Right,'" Campbell said that his work mirrors "the Christian anarchy Vernard Eller and Jacques Ellul so ably describe."[48]

Thus, despite Campbell's rejection of particular paradigms, his belief system is similar to the worldview of Christian anarchy. Moreover, Christian anarchy has influenced him and captures much of what Campbell believes about the relationship of God and humanity, as well as his present sentiments about religiously-oriented social activism.

What is Christian anarchy? The two people cited by Campbell are among the very few who have written recently on this obscure topic. One of Jacques Ellul's first treatments of anarchy was a 1980 article in Campbell's magazine, *Katallagete*.[49] This article influenced In his 1987 book, *Christian Anarchy: Jesus' Primacy Over the Powers*, Vernard Eller expanded "Ellul's insight into a thesis regarding

---

[48]*New Oxford Review*, October 1991, 7-8. Ellul, a law historian at the University of Bordeaux, combined Marxist thought and theology to offer a critique of western society. The author of forty books, Ellul died in 1994. Eller taught religion for many years at the University of La Verne in California. An ordained minister in the Church of the Brethren, Eller's numerous writings in Christian ethics advocate a progressive social agenda motivated by an explicitly religious worldview.

[49]Jacques Ellul, "Anarchism and Christianity," *Katallagete*, Fall 1980, 14-24.

Christian history."[50] A year later Ellul published the French edition of *Anarchy and Christianity*, which was translated into English in 1991. Ellul essentially expanded the work of his earlier article, and commended Eller's treatment of the subject.[51] Eller contended that

> Ellul demonstrates decisively that a particular version of "anarchism" . . . is the sociopolitical stance of the entire Bible in general and the New Testament in particular. I would add that, from there, the understanding was picked up by that church tradition perhaps most identified with "radical discipleship". . . .[52]

By anarchy, Eller did not mean political anarchy. That is, Eller did not argue that political and other institutions should be dismantled and that people should live in complete autonomy. Rather, Eller dealt with the word "anarchy" etymologically. "Archy" is the Greek root, used often in the New Testament and translated "priority, primacy, primordial, principal, prince, and the like." The prefix "an" parallels "un," and it means "not," rather than "anti." Etymologically, Eller argued that anarchy does not mean anti-government. The word refers to transcending government or political ideology for a different set of ultimate loyalties. While many forces claim ultimate loyalty—"governments . . . , philosophies, ideologies, social standards,"—the New Testament claims that God is the only force of ultimate loyalty and primacy.

> "Anarchy" . . . is simply the state of being unimpressed with, disinterested in, skeptical of, nonchalant toward, and uninfluenced by the . . . claims of any and all arkys. And

---

[50]Vernard Eller, *Christian Anarchy: Jesus' Primacy Over the Powers* (Grand Rapids: William B. Eerdmans Publishing Company, 1987), 5.

[51]"For a detailed study [of Christian anarchy] I recommend the excellent work of Vernard Eller." Ellul, *Anarchy and Christianity* (Grand Rapids: William B. Eerdmans Publishing Company, 1991), 7-8, passim.

[52]Eller, 5.

"Christian Anarchy" . . . is a Christianly motivated "unarkyness." Precisely because Jesus is THE ARKY . . . Christians dare never grant a human arky the primacy it claims for itself.[53]

In addition to claiming that his argument rests on scripture and parallels Ellul's arguments, Eller also noted similar themes in the work of Karl Barth, Søren Kierkegaard, J. C. and Christoph Blumhardt, and Dietrich Bonhoeffer. This perspective on ultimate loyalty has several implications. First, the Christian community does not withdraw from society, but rather acts only in its "own peculiarly Christian way." Second, the Christian community understands the limits of human action by recognizing the human potential to do wrong. Eller wrote that the Church rejects "the unfounded confidence in the moral competency of human beings." Finally, Christian anarchy as an approach to social action resists the taking sides with one party or cause and opposing all those with opposite views.

[T]here is another form of politics—another form of action affecting the *polis*—that the gospel can fully approve. . . . Rather than taking sides, this politics would be nonpartisanly critical of all adversary contest and power play. It would be a politics of servant ministry completely ignoring party lines—a politics intent on mediation and the reconciling of adversaries instead of supporting the triumph of one over another.[54]

Campbell agreed with this approach. His hesitancy to acknowledge specific theological influences is not an attempt to claim creativity or to evade the discovery of any links. Rather, Campbell sees theological systems as one more self-perpetuating structure, to which he does not want to lend his support. Theology is a means

---

[53]Ibid., 1-2.
[54]Ibid., xi-xiii.

to an end, but it often becomes an end in itself in Campbell's perception, and he does not want to contribute to that development.

Despite his reluctance to name theological influences, Campbell has been uncommonly open to admitting not only an affinity for the thought of Ellul, but his debt to him. "I'm accused of being heavily influenced," Campbell said, "by Jacques Ellul at this point [political action], which is alright."[55] In *Up to Our Steeples in Politics*, Campbell affirmed "the basic accuracy of the social analyses of Jacques Ellul." He particularly agreed with Ellul's contention that secular politics was not about "an exchange of ideas in political debates," but about the acquisition of power for the sake of power alone.[56]

> I do think that [I agree with] what Jacques Ellul [has written]. I have a lot of respect for him because he has been able to articulate stuff which I have suspected and thought for a long time.

While Ellul first wrote of anarchy per se in his 1980 article, the concept of Christian anarchy or transcending ideologies runs through many of his works. However, it is Vernard Eller's book, *Christian Anarchy*, that Campbell believed best expressed the proper role of the Christian community in society. Like Eller, Campbell distinguished between the political notion of anarchy and the biblical concept. The political notion of anarchy, which is opposed to and often engaged in the actual disruption of society, is the common usage of the term. The biblical notion of anarchy, according to Campbell, rests on an etymological understanding of the word. Anarchy as a biblical concept means that the worldview of the New Testament rejects any human position as deserving ultimate allegiance. "About as near as I can come," Campbell offers, "it's a sort of synonym for grace." By that, Campbell means

---

[55]Second interview by author.
[56]*Up to Our Steeples in Politics*, 112.

that anarchy related to the other biblical theme he embraces: God's universal acceptance of human beings in spite of their beliefs or backgrounds. Such divine acceptance imposes requirements other than loyalty to God above all other objects of commitment. No system should be given ultimate allegiance, especially a religious system that demands that allegiance in order to have access to God. Those who operate out of a Christian worldview, Campbell argued, "live on a different level, [and with] a different set of relationships."[57]

While he did not use the term "Christian anarchy," Campbell's reflections on the 1960s activism of the churches nonetheless reveal an anarchist perspective. That is, Campbell believed that the churches had placed too much emphasis on political solutions. He complained that religious social activists engaged in politics with utopian pretensions. He made these observations in the early 1970s, believing that the end of legal segregation had hardly integrated society or the churches. Campbell's judgment of the failure of the civil rights movement and the politically active church leaders overstates the case. The 1960s did begin with much optimism, while the period ended with a measure of corporate despair. Campbell was a product of this period, beginning the decade as a conventional activist and ending it with despair. In some ways, his judgment on the failure of the social movements of his day paralleled the despair held by many other activists. The dark events of the late 1960s blinded many to the very real gains of the era.

Campbell felt that the churches' over-reliance on politics stemmed from the "illusion that . . . politics is redemptive." Politics had ceased to be a means to an end for many in the religious community and had become an end in itself. The

---

[57]Second interview by author. Campbell became exposed to Ellul in the 1960s when the Frenchman "was first being introduced in this country [The United States]." Ellul "never got the standing that he should in the theological community. I think he's just too tough for us. We just don't want to hear what he's saying."

churches in their activism had become one more force in society competing for power and certain agendas. The presence of churches and religious organizations in social activism did not trouble Campbell. What troubled him was the "worship of politics—not politics itself." This attitude was the opposite of the distinct message of Christianity as Campbell understood it, a message that held all human solutions to be approximate.

What the religious community needed, Campbell argued, was a different understanding of proper relation of churches to political action. Campbell did not suggest that rejecting politics as "redemptive" meant a withdrawal from a public role for the churches. Rather, the churches should find a balance between investing all or no energy in the social sphere. This balance comes from recognizing the relative, temporal value of political solutions to human problems.

> Politics, as a minimum, is the means whereby we organize relatively, externally, and provisionally, the relations among men [humans]. . . . That is what political activity should make its order of business—those external, relative, provisional arrangements which deal with social and economic and political inequities and injustices.[58]

Political solutions to social problems deal with external, legal problems. These types of issues should be of some concern to the churches, but they should not be the sole concern. Political action deals only with "the adjustment of . . . laws and institutions so that they function as instruments of social justice for all." The Church was right to challenge the legalized segregation of the South, but it was wrong to assume that legalized segregation was the only problem. Indeed, Campbell contended that from a Christian perspective segregation was a symptom of a larger problem. Removing the symptom was just and noble, but it did not solve all the problems that existed among people. In other

---

[58]*Up to Our Steeples in Politics*, 69, 67.

words, many of the social ills of society are more than matters of unjust laws. The problem of racism is a theological problem. A change in the law does not end alienation between whites and African Americans.[59]

Campbell viewed the churches' vesting of all hope in political solutions as a kind of "political messianism." Here one acted "as if one more civil rights bill [on the Left] . . . [or] one more stance against 'communism' [on the Right] . . . will do it and the Kingdom of God, the Great Society, [or] Scientific Humanism will be here." Campbell believed that the churches, as well as he himself through the early 1960s, had approached their efforts in social action in this manner. The churches saw social activism as dealing with more than simply external problems. That false perspective, according to Campbell, was the reason that legal segregation could be ended while racial problems remained.

Campbell's critique of the political action of the church and the fact that few heeded his raises the question of his relationship to those within the institution. While many young ministers within the churches admire him and agree with his theology, they rarely emulate him. Indeed, to remain within the institutional church is to reject a key aspect of Campbell's religious expression. Campbell serves the institutional church as a detached voice, offering criticism that is provocative yet rarely heeded. His assessment of politics and the church illustrates the point.

"What is wrong with us that can be solved by politics," Campbell warned, "is not all that is wrong with us." Humans have problems that are greater than any simple external arrangement can solve. Moreover, problems that are political in nature and solution cannot be "cured" if Christian social activists "persist in the illusion that politics can cure everything."[60]

In *Up to Our Steeples in Politics*, Campbell concluded that political action was limited in it could deliver. By failing to recognize those limits, political activists, especially religious

---

[59]Ibid.
[60]Ibid., 70-71.

activists, limited their effectiveness by raising false expectations. When the churches engaged in political activity with utopian claims, they supported "unfilled promises [that could] only exacerbate minority alienation and majority impatience and frustration."

> This argument is one very important reason why the very proper political . . . efforts in the so-called civil rights era failed. . . . The ideology of the left and the right, conservative and liberal, drew strength from the same myth [that politics solves all problems].[61]

This attitude towards politics as a redemptive force was a great danger to the churches not only for the false hopes that it generated among the dispossessed but also because it caused the churches to trade in their unique insight for the perspective of the secular world. "The State and culture," Campbell warned, now "define all issues and rules and fields of battle. The Church then tries to do what the State, without the Church's support, had already decided to do."[62]

Campbell wanted to demonstrate that the Church had something more than political solutions to offer the larger human community. The State, or politics, or any other human institution is not "the final arbiter in the affairs between man and man [human groups]."[63] Campbell's return to a more explicitly Christian worldview meant reassessing his "hope." "I don't have any political hope," Campbell commented. His ultimate allegiance and his ultimate source of improving relationships among humans lay beyond human solutions. His "hope" was in his understanding of God.[64]

---

[61]Ibid., 113.
[62]Ibid., 3.
[63]Ibid., 66.
[64]Dibble interview, 175-177.

Rather than being shaped by any contemporary political view, Campbell hopes to transcend ideologies and seeks to begin his approach to social problems with the teachings of Jesus. This desire reflects the Christian anarchy of Eller and Ellul. Campbell made a conscious decision to relieve human suffering without regard to any particular agenda, especially that of formal conservatism or liberalism. Writing in the *New Oxford Review*, Campbell listed several of his activities, which spanned such diverse interests as his early work in civil rights, his work to raise defense funds for a Klansman on trial, his opposition to abortion, his aid to Vietnam War resisters, and his opposition to the death penalty. In taking these positions, Campbell saw himself as relieving the suffering of dispossessed people, not as responding to an ideology.

> I have never understood who sets the parameters into which we must all fit. I don't trust them and don't acknowledge their lines. I have never tried to be politically correct.[65]

Campbell took none of these actions as "political acts," rejecting the urge to compartmentalize them into right or left orientations. To do so is to accept "Caesar's [government], and society's, nomenclature," which Campbell claimed is "irrelevant" to the Christian community.[66] Believing that "persons are sovereign over principles and institutions and ideologies," Campbell determined appropriate service to be wherever persons suffer, regardless of their political orientation. Campbell took this attitude because he believed that it was "the way Christ was and is with the men [humans] of the world."[67] Thus, Campbell has not reached out to prisoners or Klansmen or other marginal groups out of a desire to arouse people's emotions. He is not merely a gadfly moving from one issue to another. In actively engaging in ethical

---

[65]*New Oxford Review*, 7.
[66]Ibid.
[67]*Up to Our Steeples*, 3-5, 12.

action, Campbell is motivated by a concern to relieve human suffering, a concern that he feels should be the fundamental motive of the people in the churches.

Campbell saw this new orientation as a return to the best of his sectarian upbringing. Again using the language of "conversion," he said that he was "converted to what is very basic to the Christian faith. . . . You can't choose who you're going to love."[68]

With this move into Christian anarchy, Campbell's evaluation of what constituted successful activism changed. Not only was he not concerned with whether his actions were of the right or left, he was also not concerned with whether his actions built a better society. The creation of a better society, for Campbell, was not relevant to the Church. Asked if he thought his approach could stabilize society, Campbell responded, "That's not for me to judge."

> When I was baptized and ordained or called, it wasn't to be effective, [it] was to be faithful. As to how well I live, I let I AM [Yahweh] be the judge.[69]

To move beyond ideology, then, is to be motivated by expressly sectarian concerns, according to Campbell. The requirement of a Christian as a Christian is "only . . . to live the whole of our lives so that it corresponds to . . . what God had done for us all in Christ."[70] This claim that the churches have no interest in building a better society is not strictly a return to a personal, privatized religious faith. Rather, Campbell is drawing a sharp distinction between the concerns of human society and what should be the concerns of the Christian Church. The Church, he believes, does not have as its primary function the building of a better human society.

---

[68]Bowman interview, 29.

[69]Second interview by author.

[70]*Up to Our Steeples in Politics*, 5.

Moving beyond ideology keeps one free of false concerns about the future, while remaining focused on the present. The future of human society is "not relevant to faith." A religious activist "should be directed toward the present" in an existential sense, with the belief that whatever takes place beyond life is beyond the immediate concern of the church.[71] Campbell's attempt to transcend ideology—to move beyond "Left, Right, or Center"—is what he considers the "essential message of Jesus."[72]

> Thus my seeming contradictions . . . reflect an effort to survive as a human being, free of other archies which inevitably define a channel in which its adherents must swim or be excluded, and which, by nature, are enslaving, for they claim ultimate allegiance.[73]

That Campbell is fully non-ideological, of course, is an exaggeration. To accept a position of Christian anarchy is itself a position. Indeed, to claim that one rests one's motivations on the teachings of Jesus is to embrace an ideological position. Moreover, many embrace the role of the church in society with less apocalyptic views and a more optimistic worldview. It is possible to take such an approach from an expressly Christian worldview.

While Campbell has categorized his Christian anarchy as reflective of the teaching of Christ, a more accurate assessment is to view Campbell's sectarian, anarchist ethics as his personal interpretation of the teachings of Christ. Nonetheless, his approach is rooted in religious thought. By embracing ideas and actions that reflect Christian anarchy, Campbell has shown himself to be more than a disillusioned social activist. His thought reflects an effort to express ethics in a contemporary age.

---

[71]Bowman interview, 39.
[72]*New Oxford Review*, 8.
[73]Ibid.

Campbell's Neo-Orthodoxy

Will Campbell is not a formal theologian. He is a minister by training and a writer by choice. He is, however, aware of theological trends beyond popular religious expressions. Although his writings are not systematic treatises, they do deal with religious questions and reflect the concerns of Campbell's faith perspective. Despite his effort to avoid indebtedness to any theological system, certain theological categories stand out. Several neo-orthodox themes occur in his writings.

What is neo-orthodoxy? The question can be almost as broad as, "What is Christianity?" Despite the breadth of the question, it is possible to list some key neo-orthodox themes that appear to epitomize the movement.[74] Neo-orthodoxy was a response to the dominant Liberal theology of the nineteenth century that still prevailed in mainline American churches by the 1920s. Liberalism, also a broad term, was an attempt to reconcile Christian thought with the advances modern culture. Perhaps the key idea that linked the various Liberal thinkers was the immanence of God, linked to an optimistic belief in inevitable social progress. Moreover, Liberalism closely identified itself with the prevailing culture. In other words, God's work was inherent in the European and American culture. The Social Gospel movement was the ethical movement that most reflected this theology.

In Europe, the events of World War I brought an end to this unbridled optimism. The cultures of the opponents were ostensibly Christian, and many religious leaders of the opposing nations endorsed the war as necessary to bring in Christian civilization. The aftermath of the war, however, shattered the notion of

---

[74]"If those who have been designated as Neo-Orthodox constituted no formal school or party, they did share a common core of postliberal assumptions." *Encyclopedia of the American Religious Experience: Studies of Traditions and Movements* (New York: Charles Scribner's Sons, 1988), s.v. "Neo-Orthodoxy," by Dennis N. Voskuil.

inevitable progress. Out of this despair grew a movement to return to traditional Christian theological categories, a movement called neo-orthodoxy. Karl Barth's 1918 commentary on Romans was in many ways the first major statement, which called the generation "back to the strange world of the Bible." By the 1930s, Barth was expanding this idea in *Church Dogmatics*, while Emil Brunner and others espoused similar ideas in what has been called the "theology of crisis."[75] Neo-orthodoxy became prominent in the United States in the 1920s and 1930s under the leadership of such thinkers as Walter Lowrie, H. Richard Niebuhr, and Reinhold Niebuhr. One of the first great statements of neo-orthodox thought in America came in a series of articles entitled, "How My Mind Has Changed," which *The Christian Century* published in 1939. Thirty-two of the contributors that year mentioned the influence of Barth and Brunner, noting their own shifts away from traditional Liberalism.

These thinkers were hardly fundamentalists, however. They attempted to respond to modern culture without a wholesale embrace of cultural values.[76] In many ways, they aimed at correcting certain perceived excesses in Liberalism without becoming reactionary. In making these correctives, several characteristically neo-orthodox themes recur. Indeed, these themes can be labeled as basic tenets of neo-orthodoxy. One idea is a return to a belief in the sinfulness of humanity, especially as that idea is expressed in the works of Paul, Augustine, Luther, and Calvin.[77] Second, neo-orthodoxy emphasized the transcendence or otherness of God. This emphasis was not a complete rejection of the immanence of God, for neo-orthodoxy retained a strong incarnational theology.

---

[75]Sydney Ahlstrom, *A Religious History of the American People*, vol. II (New Haven: Yale University Press, 1972; Image Books, 1975), 426-427.

[76]Daniel Reid, et al., eds, *Dictionary of Christianity in America* (Downers Grove, Illinois: Intervarsity Press, 1990), S.v. "Neo-Orthodoxy," by D. K. McKim.

[77]Voskuil, 1154; Ahlstrom, 442. Neo-orthodox theology "above all [called for] the full restoration of Saint Paul as the first Doctor of the Church." Ibid.

Rather, the emphasis was a means of retaining the distinction between God on the one hand, and human culture on the other.

Neo-orthodoxy also eagerly returned to the language of the Bible as the starting point for theology. This emphasis was not a return to literalism. Rather, it was a return to a belief that God communicated to humans in a unique and primary fashion through the biblical texts.

Finally, neo-orthodoxy reassessed the role of the churches in social action. While the movement did not reject the value of working to improve society, the new doctrinal correctives of the movement necessitated a more tempered approach to these efforts. No longer did these people believe that the social efforts of Christians would create the Kingdom of God on Earth. Rather, neo-orthodoxy stressed the relative nature of social action, with a belief that human actions are only approximate solutions.[78]

These general themes of neo-orthodoxy appear in Campbell's thought. After his own self-examination in the 1960s, his writings reflect an emphasis on human sinfulness or potential for evil, the sinfulness of human institutions, a criticism of liberal optimism, the otherness of God, and a call for a return to scriptural ideas as the starting point for Christian social action.

Campbell holds to a strong concept of human sin, especially the sinfulness or potential evil in human structures or institutions. Indeed, he sees the biggest threat to the Church as those posed by the institutions created by the church. How does he define an institution? Campbell defined an institution as "an organization set up to meet the continuing needs of a group." Because of that definition, and his belief in the sinfulness of humanity, he concluded that the institution must be sinful as well. Campbell has been clear about his understanding of human sin, and how individual sinfulness translates into corporate sin.

---

[78]For a detailed description of neo-orthodoxy, see Ahlstrom, McKim, and Voskuil.

Now the doctrine of original sin portrays man [humanity] as self-loving, self-serving, egotistical, and thinking more highly of himself than those around him. Therefore, if something is set up to meet those continuing kinds of needs, then it [the institution] is inherently evil.

Campbell decided that if one cannot accept the corporate dimensions of sin, "then we just don't understand the Christian doctrine of man [humanity] in the first place."[79] While a movement may start out with the best of motives, ultimately it will become institutionalized, and with that process will come the sinfulness that Campbell criticizes. No institution was free of the potential for evil. Indeed, Campbell held the inherent sinfulness of an institution to be more pervasive than that of an individual. Unlike an individual, an institution cannot be redeemed. He believed that this idea had been confirmed in his own experiences. Institutions are "all after your soul, after your ultimate allegiance, and they get it one way or another, or you're out."[80]

Campbell recognized institutional structures as necessary realities. While he saw no inherent value in a structure, he recognized their value as pragmatic means to an end. His sense of corporate sin did not call for withdrawal. He affirmed the work that individuals do through institutions, and admitted, "I work within them all the time. I don't claim not to." His approach, though, avoided ultimate allegiance to any structure. Campbell did not want to value the work of an institution to the point of viewing it as inherently good. Rather than withdrawing from it, his perspective has been, "I'm working within this particular institution . . . but I don't trust you."[81] On the other hand, he called for a sense of humility regarding institutional structures. Institutions,

---

[79]Bowman interview, 31.

[80]Second interview by author. Of the possibility of creating a Christian society, Campbell said, "There never has been one yet. Calvin thought that there is a Christian state, and I don't believe in that." Dibble interview, 176.

[81]McNabb interview, 14.

once established, have a way of sensing that they are irreplaceable. Long after the original cause of their founding has ended, the organizations remain. Campbell believed this to be the case of the Southern Christian Leadership Conference, which he felt was essentially a forum for the work of Martin Luther King. The SCLC "should have folded when he died," according to Campbell. Campbell held similar sentiments about Koinonia Farm, the communal, interracial farm started by Clarence Jordan.

The institutional church is not exempt from corporate sin. The churches have been some of the most infamous examples of human depravity, according to Campbell. He especially contended that traditional religion's concern with dogma, rather than ethical action, indicated corporate sin. Institutional religion has equated "belief with faith. Belief is not faith. The devils believe." Hence, he views "the inquisitions, the holy wars, and the modern day internal warfare within denominations like the Southern Baptists" as matters of belief, not faith.[82]

Campbell's sense of corporate sin did not soften his belief in the sinfulness of individuals. He believed that all individuals were potentially self-serving and egocentric. Moreover, he thought that the religious social activists, including himself, had been deluded by an overly optimistic view of human nature. Religious leaders had failed to present a comprehensive message of humanity because of this optimism. While some might argue that the churches did not sufficiently emphasize the value of all persons, in *Race and the Renewal of the Church*, Campbell dealt at length with issues of human nature. He held that the value of all humans "has been said sweetly and often enough." The problem of the churches "is that we have spoken too much of man's worth and dignity and not often enough of his insignificance in God's scheme of things." The message of the churches should be that human beings are "all undeserving, yet loved and accepted of God, our common father."

The overly optimistic doctrine of humanity hampered the work of the religious social activists because it made them naive.

---

[82]Second interview by author.

Campbell believed that many social activists emphasized the judgment of God only on the segregationist. Human depravity, however, "is not a message for the majority group alone."

> The disease exists just as acutely in the minority group as it does in the majority. It is no startling thing to say that original sin is not peculiar to white people. . . . We were bringing one message to the prejudiced and another to the victims of prejudice. The message is not divided. The sins are the same in both groups.[83]

All persons have the potential for evil. Merely eliminating legal barriers to racial segregation would not improve race relations. Many social activists, according to Campbell, had placed too much hope in the civil rights movement, without accepting a belief in the movement's tendency toward sinfulness. "The liberal church people in the sixties," according to Campbell, [had a tendency] to overly romanticize the movement and assume that if someone were black, they looked like Lena Horne and thought like Thurgood Marshall."[84]

Like many neo-orthodox thinkers, Campbell reassessed the importance of the Social Gospel, which was in many ways a precursor to the civil rights movement. He did not criticize Walter Rauschenbusch, but he did criticize the methods taken by the institutional church to implement Rauschenbusch's ideas. He went so far as to say, "Those second and third generation disciples have wandered far away from the Christian faith." Campbell's greatest concern with the heirs of the Social Gospel was their overly optimistic doctrine of humanity. The Social Gospel "assumed that all men are good and would live accordingly if they could just be taught."

Campbell also faulted the Social Gospel and its contemporary heirs for attempting to "build a kingdom in which it will be

---

[83]*Race and the Renewal of the Church*, 33, 47, 60.
[84]Second interview by author.

possible for men [humanity] to live as brothers [and sisters]." He faulted this notion not only because of his understanding of human depravity, but also because he saw that goal as beyond the legitimate goal of the Christian religion. Creating the Kingdom of God on earth "is very fine sociologically and politically, but it's not Christian." Social activism of this type, according to Campbell, started with cultural values and imposed them on the Christian message. Likewise, Campbell faulted this type of social action for "putting man [humanity] at the center of the universe. . . . The Christian faith should put God at the center of the universe."[85] Campbell's language and social ethic at this point sound like an escapist and individualistic—and almost fundamentalist—world-view. The harsh tone, however, is hyperbolic. Campbell's critique of the Social Gospel reflects Neo-Orthodoxy in popular thought.

The sovereignty of God also plays a prominent role in the thought of Will Campbell. He believed that the religious community should be motivated to action by a sense of God's sovereignty, rather than by "some illusion about creating a kingdom."[86] The work of Campbell's contemporary social activists had lost its emphasis on the otherness of God. Again in *Race and the Renewal of the Church,* he argues that religion had shifted from a belief in the otherness of God to the "potential divinity in every man [human]." With this change came an emphasis on Jesus becoming God rather than God becoming a man. Campbell meant by this charge that the Christian religion, especially in its social expression, was anthropocentric, rather than theocentric. For Campbell, this shift placed too much worth in the actions of human beings.

> Theological liberalism . . . interpreted Jesus as a rebel prophet [who became God] as a reward for the life he lived and the deeds he had performed. . . . The meaning of the crucifixion and death of Christ is completely changed by

---

[85]Bowman interview, 30, 39.
[86]"White Liberals—All Right in their Place," *Social Progress*, December 1963, 30.

this theology. One of its most serious consequences is the rejection of the doctrine of the absolute sovereignty of God.

Many of the problems in race relations stemmed from an inadequate doctrine of God's sovereignty, according to Campbell. The anthropocentric approach started with the wrong point of reference. Anthropocentrism not only could not solve racial problems, it could exacerbate them. Part of the reason people were racist—or committed other injustices—was because of their self-centeredness. Racism is "an effort to deny the sovereignty of God," and the problem could only be addressed by first affirming God's sovereignty.

> [T]he sovereignty of God . . . is the beginning and the end of Christian race relations. It is only by beginning with God that we get a true perspective for the understanding of man [humanity].[87]

Campbell's strong emphasis on the sovereignty of God not only resembles but is connected to the thought of Karl Barth. In addition to sovereignty, Campbell called for the increased use of biblical language, often quoting Barth. In *Race and the Renewal of the Church*, Campbell proposed that scripture is theocentric, rather than anthropocentric, and he credited Barth with making that observation known to the modern church.

> The Biblical writers . . . as Karl Barth has so often pointed out, were concerned with what God thinks about man. Their account makes God the subject and man [humanity] the object.[88]

Campbell also lamented the close association of Christian thought with modern, democratic culture. He saw this identifica-

---

[87]*Race and the Renewal of the Church*, 53, 55, and 58.
[88]Ibid., 57-58.

tion as part of the reason that biblicism was not more prevalent among white civil rights activists. Many religious social activists, Campbell argued, believe that ideas "from the infantile world of the Bible must be filtered through . . . the mature world of the twentieth century." For Campbell, this assumption was a mistake. He felt that the starting place for social action was in the Bible." Moreover, he rejected the view that modern culture was closer to the divine ideal.

> [Those] who glory in and celebrate their modernity are unwilling to acknowledge the relative, historical quality of the ideas about faith and life which the twentieth century shares with the sixteenth or first centuries.[89]

By embracing "biblicism," Campbell saw himself as following the tradition of Karl Barth. While Barth may not have been the single influence causing Campbell to return to a strong, religiously oriented worldview, Barth's thought reinforced Campbell in this direction. By being Pauline and biblicist, Campbell said that he meant what "Karl Barth meant forty years ago when he explained that his 'biblicism' consisted in . . . supposing the Bible to be a good book . . . [and that people] should take its conceptions as seriously as they take their own."

Campbell argued that social activists must not take their own ideas and then look to scripture to reinforce those ideas. He criticized this error in both his contemporary revolutionaries and reactionaries. Such a mistake fails to consider seriously the "conceptions" of scripture, distorting its "authoritative character and quality."[90] Again alluding to Barth, Campbell said that the Bible does not speak of creating "any kind of society" in the larger secular world. He believed that the message of scripture is that one should make a Christian response in whatever circumstances one may be. Campbell referred to Barth's advice to Germans in the

---

[89]*Up to Our Steeples in Politics*, 8-9.
[90]Ibid.

Nazi era when he said the Church should live as if the Nazis did not exist. Quoting this statement, Campbell thought Barth meant that "a Christian has got to be the same whether or not he [an enemy] is going to cut your head off."[91] A consistent response, in Campbell's thinking, results from a biblically-ground ed worldview, rather than a culturally-centered worldview.

Campbell does not resist the Barthian label, though he admitted never having read more than some forty pages of Barth in his life, and Barthian ideas do seem to appear in Campbell's writings. If Campbell has read very little of Barth, it seems that the small amount has had a large influence.[92]

Finally, Campbell's thought resembles neo-orthodoxy in its reaffirmation of the unique character and language of the Church. What he considered the failures of the churches in social action could be corrected not by a more modern worldview, nor by a return to "revivalism," but by "a well-defined orthodoxy."[93] When he spoke to the Centennial Conference on Race and Religion, he made a similar claim, reminding the audience that it was present primarily as Jews and Christians, not as civil libertarians.[94]

Campbell felt that the churches had adopted the dominant, progressive elements in culture to guide them, acting "as if they, God's ambassadors, had nothing to say as God's ambassadors about man's nature and destiny."[95] The churches, however, had much to say out of their own traditions, and Campbell thought these traditions should be the unique contribution of the religious community to social action. Christian social action should speak "in the Church's own peculiar message, using its own language and

---

[91]Caudill interview, 91.

[92]Second interview by author. Campbell does not admit to reading large numbers of books, magazines, or newspapers on a regular basis. He does not read widely, he claims, because he is "a slow reader." "I don't read a lot. . . . [T]his guy that . . . went to seminary with me says that Will Campbell's written more books than he's read. But I'm not proud of that. I am a very slow reader."

[93]*Up to Our Steeples in Politics*, 18.

[94]"The Inner Life of Church and Synagogue," 15.

[95]*Up to Our Steeples in Politics*, 115.

its own frame of reference." The churches needed to provide a missing element in social activism: "a positive theological base."[96]

One of the motivations for writing *Race and the Renewal of the Church* is implied in the title. Campbell thought that the churches, despite their numerous statements and efforts on social issues, had approached the issues with theological deficiency. He did not want the churches to withdraw, but to speak in their own language, which he said would strengthen their own unique character. He lamented that the churches had taken a nonsectarian, humanist approach to the race issue, with a larger concern for reforming society than for renewing its character. The "voice [of the church] has been too often an echo of the cry for law and order, democracy, the rights of man, human dignity, constitutional process, the public schools." Campbell sees such concerns as fine in themselves but notes that they are not the church's essential concern.[97] The Church, Campbell's arguments notwithstanding, *does* have an interest in enlightenment concepts such as civil rights or human dignity. If there is no legitimate, religious argument that an African American should have the right to vote, then churches hardly have any grounds to protest the denial of certain rights. While the starting point of the churches in social activism should be rooted in religious concerns, their decision to enter the public arena should have some basis in the shared concerns of the society. Speaking in the language of shared concerns prevents a religious organization from imposing its dogma on society. To say that the Church should speak in its own voice is a legitimate challenge, but that challenge does not sufficiently prepare the Church to engage in society.

Campbell's criticism of the Church's use of a secular approach to social issues was not a criticism of that approach. He approved of the actions of the non-sectarian groups. Campbell acknowledged the debt owed to humanism's egalitarianism. But he argued that a

---

[96]"The Role of Religion in the Desegregation Controversy," *Union Seminary Quarterly Review* 16 (January 1961): 191-192.

[97]*Race and the Renewal of the Church*, 4.

secular approach did not accord with the biblical message on race, which to Campbell transcends "egalitarian premises and arguments." In the Christian community, Campbell argued, people should spend their energy moving people, black and white, beyond racial awareness.

The churches, however, had not focused on self-renewal, nor had they taken the lead in race relations in specifically religious terms. By this approach, the churches had added little to social action and had diluted their unique character. When the churches approach social issues from the point of law, rights, or democracy,

> Our churches . . . become adjuncts to human relations councils and civil rights organizations, . . . but this is to sell what we have much too short. For what we have to say is far more radical, far more demanding, far more inclusive of all of society than anything the humanistically oriented groups have said.[98]

Moreover, the use of a secular orientation by the churches alters the nature of the ministry. The churches no longer speak in a distinct voice. They become "inclined to look for effective, skilled social reformers or human engineers, but rarely preachers and prophets."

When one takes a position on social action based on secular thought, the issue is subject to debate because of the finite knowledge of humanity. Human analyses are subject to change. For example, Campbell argued that many church leaders called for desegregation out of obedience to the 1954 Supreme Court ruling. Even that ruling, however, should not have been as imposing on the churches as "a bold position based on the Christian doctrine of man [humanity], the Biblical imperative of justice, and doctrine of the sovereignty of God."

That the churches had lost their theological orientation was evident in that the churches waited until the Supreme Court ruling

---

[98]Ibid., 39, 36-37.

of 1954 to engage in race relations. Campbell saw this delay as following the culture, rather than speaking to the culture. The delay not only hampered the effectiveness of the churches but also hurt the nature of the churches. Losing its distinctiveness, "the Church seems to offer nothing more than its institutional form as a vehicle to accomplish ends motivated by an alien philosophy."[99]

> [T]he witness of the Church can only be to repent of its failure in the process of desegregation and move with its own particular and peculiar message of redemption into the process of true integration, reconciliation, renewal, a job neither the courts, secular agencies, nor direct action movements can accomplish.[100]

Using a more distinctively Christian approach, with more dependence on the language and thought of scripture, would also have a pragmatic value. The segregationist of the South, according to Campbell, was often a very religious person. Appealing to this person on the basis of civil rights or law was of little value. Indeed this person often thought the Bible endorsed segregation, and that the state laws upholding segregation were divinely sanctioned. The racist, in Campbell's estimation, "defends white supremacy in God's name"; thus, the solution lies in reforming that person's understanding of God, rather than appealing to him or her on the basis of the law.[101]

This solution, however, addresses the problem of racism in the churches, not in society. From several points of view, an exclusively religious approach to the issue is inadequate. First, the problems of the society at large were legitimate problems related to legalized segregation. The society could not begin to have any sense of racial equality without a change in laws. Second, while the churches

---

[99]Ibid., 37, 28, 70.

[100]"Rumblings of Rebellion by Southern White Clergy," *Dialogue* 3 (Spring 1964): 126.

[101]"A Man Had Two Sons," *Christianity Today*, 10 April 1964, 36.

could affect the culture in a positive role, it is also likely that the cultural and legal changes could affect the churches. People who reinforce their racism with religion are inclined to reconsider aspects of their religion as they see less of their religiously oriented beliefs reflected in state laws. Put a different way, whites who drink from the same fountain and eat in the same restaurants with African Americans may not integrate their churches, but they will reassess their understanding of the divine sanction of segregation.

Campbell believed that by neglecting its distinctive message, the Church made a great tactical mistake in its efforts to fight racism. The southern segregationist is convinced that his or her views are biblical. The more effective strategy would be to speak to them in explicitly religious terms. Campbell concluded that segregationists are not motivated by appeals to law or civil rights since they reject those categories. Just as the religious segregationist believes that legal separation of the races is divinely ordained, even so the social activist should attempt to convince that person that these views are not scriptural. The solution to racial problems lies in the "redemptive purpose of Jesus Christ and the judgment of God." The religiously oriented segregationist must be shown to be in religious error. He argued:

> Few Americans are so secularized as to have no sense of the meaning of the judgment of God upon his people. We should remember (and this is especially true in the South) that the racist is seldom an atheist.[102]

Unfortunately, it is very doubtful that a religious approach to the segregationist would have been any more effective. While those people were convinced that the Bible endorsed segregation, they did not derive their racism from religion. Rather, their racism was the heritage of their culture, which their religion reinforced. To tell segregationists that they face God's judgment rather than telling

---

[102]*Race and the Renewal of the Church*, 47.

them that their actions are unconstitutional may be a more sectarian approach to racial problems.

In all likelihood, however, the segregationist would simply dismiss the interpretation of the social activist. In many ways, the behavior of the segregationists was changed by a legal action. It was, in hindsight, much easier to convince segregationists that their practices violated the law of the land than to tell them they stood in danger of divine wrath.

To summarize, then, Will D. Campbell has been active in social work of some type since his days as a young minister in Taylor, Louisiana. After his work with the National Council of Churches, Campbell began to examine his approach to social issues. He did not change his concern for human suffering, but he saw a need for the church to address social issues in more explicitly Christian terms.

While it is difficult to categorize Campbell, his statements do appear to have been influenced by the works of Jacques Ellul, Vernard Eller, and neo-orthodoxy. Campbell is a deep, reflective thinker whose iconoclasm does not reduce him to a mere disaffected cynic. His mature thought does not reject the Christian message, but rather attempts to preach it to a culture that in his estimation contradicts the essential teachings of Jesus.

Chapter 3

Two or Three
Gathered Together:
Campbell and the Institutional Church

Despite his criticism of institutional religion, Campbell did not reject the world of faith. His understanding of the true Church, however, clashed with institutional religion. This contrast between the nature of the true community of faith and the nature of institutional religion has been one of the central themes of Campbell's mature thought. To one degree or another, all of his works of nonfiction touch this theme, as do his novels, *The Convention*, *Cecelia's Sin*, and *The Glad River*. In addressing these issues through his writings, Campbell puts forward a contemporary version of Baptist and Anabaptist understandings of the Church.

Christianity and Christendom

Will Campbell distinguishes between Christianity as authentically practiced and Christianity as an element of culture. He also held that when churches become part of the larger culture, these groups cease to be the legitimate heirs of the teachings of Jesus. Ecclesiology has to do with the nature and form of the Church. According to many students of ecclesiology, the Church can be understood in five dimensions: worship, teaching, work, polity, and function. Worship refers to the liturgical expression of the Church; teaching refers to its dogma; and polity is the government of the Church. Work and function as dimensions of ecclesiology are similar. The work of the Church is proclaiming the truth of Christianity through "loving service to others," while the function of the Church is "to serve the increase of love of God and neighbor."[1] In Campbell's ecclesiology or view of the Church, the nature of the Church does not involve traditional liturgy or dogma. The Church is exclusively functional. The Church exists when a person "supports others and holds them up and celebrates life and expresses hope and resurrection."[2] Indeed, these actions are the Church. Moreover, Campbell does not think that the institutional church is necessarily the location of these actions. In fact, the institutional church for Campbell is rarely the place where theses actions take place. More often than not, the institutional church inhibits the expression of Christianity.

For Campbell the close identity of the churches with culture hinders their authentic religion. That a country or culture is ostensibly Christian has nothing to do with whether that society contains true believers. Campbell draws contrasts between the Christianity of the first century Church and Christianity as expressed in the centuries after it became the dominant religion. In this regard, Campbell is a primitivist. He extols the virtues of first century Christianity and laments the decline of the Church after its first generation. Christianity as the dominant religion of a culture is Christendom and Campbell believed that Christendom and Christianity are two different things. According to Campbell, "Kierkegaard's various attacks on 'the monstrous illusion of Christendom' have more to say to us about the Church" than anything done by the institutional churches.[3]

Campbell believes that the prevalence of institutional Christianity in the United States actually hampers the expression of true Christianity. The large number of active church members in the United States did not have any bearing on the presence of true Christianity. "The problem with Christianity in our nation," Campbell told a group of ministers at Emory University, "is not that not enough people love Jesus. The problem is that everyone

---

[1]Samuel S. Hill, ed., *The Encyclopedia of Religion in the South* (Macon: Mercer University Press, 1984), s.v. "Ecclesiology," by Theron Price.

[2]Caudill interview, 99.

[3]*Up to Our Steeples in Politics*, 12.

loves Jesus." Institutional Christianity is an accepted cultural value of the United States, and this high degree of acceptance detracts from the true essence of Christianity. In other words, Campbell told them, "[T]he cross has been shined up."[4] Christendom attempts to make its structures part of the larger culture. When this attempt succeeds, the structures lose their distinctive character as expressions of the Church.

This loss occurred in the South precisely because of the region's pervasive religious atmosphere. Campbell pointed out in a 1963 speech that no major minister in the South opposed slavery by the time of the Civil War.[5] While the South was a very religious region, Campbell concluded that it was the religion of Christendom, not authentic Christianity. The 1963 speech was one of the first times that Campbell publically made this charge. Twenty-three years later, when he spoke at Emory University, Campbell made the same charge against cultural Christianity, this time leveling his accusations against the administration of President Ronald Reagan. He lamented Reagan's endorsement of a national holiday for Martin Luther King, Jr. For Campbell, Reagan's endorsement served as the quintessential example of culture religion. While Reagan's words endorsed the holiday, Campbell believed that Reagan's actions had prevented forty-six percent of African American youths from finding jobs and had forced fifteen percent of these youths into the streets.

Institutional structures of religion do not reflect authentic Christianity because their actions do not reflect their dogma. The institutional churches, as part of the culture, "proclaim . . . love for Jesus too much and too often, [and] in my judgment, we are lying."[6] Why is the typical form of Christian expression in the United States inauthentic? Because it is shaped by, rather than set apart from, culture. The true Church does not become merely another element in the culture of a society.

---

[4]"What Do We Do About What Has Been Done?" Sound recording.
[5]"The Inner Life of Church and Synagogue", 13.
[6]"What Do We Do . . ."

During his activity in the civil rights movement that Campbell decided that all American denominations were captive to the culture. The churches as a whole did not provide strong leadership in the integration crisis. Rather, the churches followed the lead of the culture. Not only did many in the churches resist integration, many of the supporters of the civil rights movement emerged after others in society forced the issue. "A ministry," Campbell argued, "cannot be prophetic if it is only now witnessing to what all institutions of culture have already accepted." He added that other segments of society "have moved far ahead of the churches."[7] His dismal assessment of the churches did not force Campbell to reject Christianity. He does, however, distinguish between authentic Christianity and its institutions. For Campbell much of the work of the institutional church contradicts the teachings of Jesus, and the form of the institutional church is not the legitimate heir of the first century church. Rather, he argues the goals contemporary churches, Christian colleges, and seminaries are blasphemous.[8]

The institutional church rarely becomes the true Church because the goals of institutional religion and the Church are often antithetical. When a challenge to the culture occurs, some form of social disruption results. The institutional churches, as part of the culture, work to preserve themselves and the culture in which they exist. They do not challenge elements of the culture. By serving this function, the institutional church will attack any threat to itself or its culture, even if the challenge comes from an element of authentic Christianity.

In making this point, Campbell has cited the example of Paul Turner, formerly pastor of First Baptist Church in Clinton, Tennessee. The Ku Klux Klan, under the leadership of John Kasper, targeted the town to fight the integration of the local schools. Violence soon erupted, including the bombing of one of the schools, and Campbell traveled to the town to encourage the white ministers to speak out against the violence. Campbell met

---

[7]"Rumblings of Rebellion Among Southern Clergy," 125.
[8]*Up to Our Steeples in Politics*, 2.

with Paul Turner, but in their conversation Turner did nothing to indicate that he would speak out on the issue. Shortly after their meeting, however, Turner escorted some African American students to the school and was attacked by a mob. As a result of his challenge to the culture, he was forced from the pulpit of First Baptist. Controversy, notes Campbell, cost Turner his pastorate.[9]

According to Campbell, this tendency toward self-preservation reflects Christendom because it attacks the source of controversy and because it rejects the ethics of Jesus. By deliberately avoiding controversy, the institutional church becomes irrelevant both to the true Church and to the culture it seeks to preserve. This idea became especially apparent to Campbell during the summer of 1961, when he spent much of his time in Montgomery, Alabama. The escalating moves for integration had elicited particularly violent responses. In the midst of the violence, Campbell often listened to the radio broadcasts of the city's white pastors, and he was struck by how little authentic Christianity he heard in their sermons. Their failure, however, was not in their opposition to integration, but in their silent response to the violence.

> I rode around that city all day in 1961, listening to sermons and I might as well have been on Mars. Here an entire city was going up almost literally in flames and in church people were going around talking about if your mother is dead wear a white rose and if she's living wear a red rose.[10]

For Campbell, this pattern of cultural accommodation by the institutional church was not a recent phenomenon. The institutional church arose shortly after the first century, he believed, culminating with the proclamation of Christianity as the official religion of the Roman Empire. Viewing church history from a sectarian, Anabaptist perspective, Campbell held that the adoption

---

[9]Caudill interview, 58-59.
[10]"Our Adolescent History," 44-45.

of Christianity as the official religion of the Roman Empire greatly weakened the moral authority of the Church. The transition of the church from a persecuted element in the culture to an integral component of the culture corrupted the nature of the institutional church. Beginning at that time, the institutional church "had hardly become distinguishable from the society in which it finds itself at any given moment in history."[11]

Campbell does not deny that religious structures at times represent the work of the Church universal, but he feels that one must not equate the institution with the Church. His understanding of the Church is almost wholly non-institutional. Although he distrusted the institutional church, Campbell admitted the possibility that the structure can occasionally represent his idea of God. Campbell said, "That doesn't mean that God doesn't work wherever God chooses, so I wouldn't rule out the stained glass and the mahogany pews and the silver chalices."[12] What Campbell opposed is the equating of the institutional church and cultural Christianity with the Church as it was originally intended to be.

In searching for terms to express his distinction between the true Church and the institution, Campbell chose to refer to the institution by the term, "steeple." Because he no longer equated the work of the "steeple" (or institution) with the work of the Church, Campbell stopped participating regularly in the institutional ministry, while still understanding himself to be involved in the work of the Church. Asked if he regularly participated in an institutional church of any kind, Campbell responded, "We could talk the rest of the day about what you mean by 'go to church.' I don't go to a steeple."[13]

Indeed, Campbell believed that the heavy reliance of the Christian community on its own structures contributed to the

---

[11]"Values and Hazards of Theological Preaching," in *The Pastor as Theologian*, eds. Earl E. Shelp and Ronald H. Sunderland, (New York: Pilgrim Press, 1988), 85.

[12]McNabb interview, 14.

[13]Second interview by author.

decline of the institutional church as a legitimate representative of the work of Jesus. When people served the Church, they were actually serving the institution and the culture and equating such service with service to God. Eventually, people equated God with the institutional church, which hampered the ability of the institution to do the work of the Church.

> We should know better than to worship the institutional church, but we keep falling into the trap. We are taught to be loyal to the church. Well, I don't love the church—not the institutional church.[14]

Campbell argues that the institutional church ceased to represent the true Church by so closely identifying with the values of culture. Many others have voiced this criticism. For example, John Lee Eighmy advanced a similar thesis in his study of Southern Baptists social attitudes, *Churches in Cultural Captivity*. Southern Baptist social views in the first half of the twentieth century were, Eighmy argued, were "more provincial and conservative" than the social attitudes of other American churches. He lists two reasons for this conservatism. First, Southern Baptists have made numerical growth a priority, which necessitates both avoiding conflict and articulating an appealing message. Second, and most important, Southern Baptist church polity, with its local control and non-hierarchical ministry, discourages ministers from challenging the status quo. In fact, the nature of the system encourages pastors to affirm the status quo.[15] Similarly, Campbell holds that in so doing the institutional church failed to be "true to its own nature."[16] Campbell first observed what he believed to be the

---

[14]Bowman interview, 31.

[15]John Lee Eighmy, *Churches in Cultural Captivity: A History of the Social Attitudes of Southern Baptists*, rev. ed., with an introduction, conclusion, and bibliography by Samuel S. Hill (Knoxville: The University of Tennessee Press, 1987), xix-xx.

[16]*Race and the Renewal of the Church*, 4.

failure of the institutional churches to represent the true Church—to be true to their nature—during the civil rights movement. He lamented that segregation could be so entrenched in a culture that was so pervasively religious. His new understanding of the nature of the Church as a distinct entity from the institutional church helped him reconcile the contradiction.

In *Race and the Renewal of the Church*, Campbell suggested that the churches do not have an inviolable position as the representative of God. Campbell allowed the possibility that God could cease to influence the churches. If the churches continued to be governed by cultural mores, often to the point of contradicting Christian ethics, these groups could "at some point . . . cease to be the church." The institutional church, both by failing to model Christian race relations at the local level and by apparently having little interest in doing so, had rejected its mission and nature.[17] Campbell did not believe that the Church had ceased to exist or that God no longer worked in the world. Rather, he believed that the Church existed wherever people engaged in ethically uplifting actions. The work of the Church can be embodied in structures other than those of the institutional churches. He warned the Conference on Race and Religion about this perceived danger.

> Perhaps God has already moved out of our houses erected
> in his name and that such inner life as we may now know
> it is but the growth of a man's beard after he has been
> placed in the casket.[18]

Campbell's criticism of the institutional church is not criticism from a secularist perspective. He did not direct his challenge to the core of Christian teaching, but rather to the failure of the institution to be true to that core. That the institutional churches might be numerically strong or culturally prevalent had nothing to do with the institution as a representative of the Church universal.

---

[17]*Ibid.*, 10-12.
[18]"The Inner Life of Church and Synagogue," 14.

"[I]n terms of working efficiently," Campbell commented, "God knows they [the institutions] work efficiently. Whether there is any kerygma there, I don't know."[19]

The presence of kerygma was doubtful, Campbell thinks, because of the dichotomy between the practice of the institutions and the teachings of Christianity. When he spoke to the Conference on Race and Religion, he pointed out the contradiction between Christian teachings on human relations and the social practices Christians, individually and collectively. The teachings of Christianity and Judaism supplied more than enough ethical grounding against racial tensions. "The traditional Shema, as old as Israel itself," Campbell told the audience, "should be enough to solve the race problem. It hasn't solved it." Likewise, he cited the portion of the Mass where the priest refers to God as a father, as well as the use of the Apostles Creed by many Protestant Churches.

> These words, the Shema, the words from the Mass, the central message of most Protestant liturgy scream out at us that . . . we are all here dying together. They alone should have been enough to teach us the error of our ways in dividing people into such categories as race. But the truth is they haven't.[20]

The institutional churches had denied their nature by failing to live in a manner consistent with their beliefs. The institutions of religion no longer represented authentic Christianity, which exists in places outside the denominations and formal expressions of Christianity. Campbell had come to doubt whether authentic Christianity could be found in the institutions.

> We must ask ourselves, earnestly and prayerfully, whether *we* are still the church. If we discover that God has turned

---

[19]Second interview by author.
[20]"The Inner Life of Church and Synagogue," 9-11.

to other vehicles, it will not be because he has left his
people, but because the people have left God.[21]

By the late 1960s and early 1970s, Campbell condemned the
institutional church even more dramatically. In one interview,
Campbell referred to the institutional church as "the greatest
obstacle to the radical proclamation of the Christian faith."[22] He
even suggested that many of the forces in mainline churches that
became involved in the integration crisis did so only when it
seemed they might otherwise lose their influence in the culture.
Quoting Kay Jones of the Tennessee Council on Human Relations,
Campbell said,

> They [the institutional churches] have left the ranks of the
> church universal. . . . They preside over weekly meetings of
> their own little country clubs. They are neither spiritual
> leaders nor do they influence the community's decision
> makers.[23]

Campbell's assessment of the institutional church is harsh and
a direct outgrowth of his own experiences. He has responded to the
institutional church as one with high expectations for the churches'
role in transforming society. His ecclesiology only took on its
anti-institutional flavor after being disappointed by the Church's
failure to relieve human suffering. Rejecting the institutional
church as an authentic expression of Christianity allowed Campbell to retain high ideals about the nature of the Church. The move
allowed him to be disillusioned with the structures of Christianity
without being disillusioned with the ethics of Christianity.
However, a historical link exists between the institutional churches
and Campbell's high ideals. Despite the failure of the institutional
churches to live up to their ideals, they are the repository of these

---

[21]*Race and the Renewal of the Church*, 9.
[22]Bowman interview, 31.
[23]"Rumblings of Rebellion Among Southern White Clergy," 126.

ideals. Without the institutions would the ideals he embraces survive?

Perhaps Campbell's strong words are hyperbolic. He made strong statements in order to emphasize his point. While he was very serious about the failure of the institutional churches to live up to their ethics, he acknowledged that institutional churches at least provide an ethical standard that will motivate some people, even if they must turn elsewhere to meet their goals. In his article, "The Role of Religion in the Desegregation Controversy," Campbell cites two illustrations.

First, Campbell notes the role of the African American church in social activism. The record of these churches was "a notable exception" to the poor record of the other churches. The African American church had not merely been active in desegregation, it had led the efforts in that community. When the African American church promoted desegregation, Campbell saw their actions as representative of the true Church.

> The meetings were not only held in church houses, they were essentially religious meetings with religious motivations and values. . . . This was the church playing a vital role in desegregation.

His judgment of the African-American church contains a certain "romanticism." Although his strong doctrine of human sin applies to this institution as much as to any other, he has concluded that even as a human institution the African American church more nearly approximates the ideals of the true Church. Campbell concluded, "I do think that as an institution it is less structured. And the historic Baptist polity is more nearly alive there than in white circles."

Campbell, second, has acknowledged the role of the institutional church in producing religiously oriented social activists. Even if these activists must eventually "deny the mother church that gave them birth," there nevertheless remains a connection between the institution and the activist. Christian-oriented social activists often received their first exposure to ethical teaching as a direct result of having been reared in the institutional church.

How could the institution produce socially active ministers and laity and yet fail to address social problems as an institution? Part of the problem stemmed from the essential character of Protestantism. American Protestantism did not have a polity that made its structural policies sufficiently binding on local congregations. The national organizations of the Protestant churches could make socially progressive statements, but they cannot transform these statements into actions. The leaders in the Protestant churches do not have the authority to enforce a decision of the clergy. For this reason, the socially progressive views of some leaders had little effect on many in the local congregations. However, some people were influenced by teachings they received within the churches. The institutional church must at least be seen as responsible for exposing people to authentic Christianity, even if it failed to exhibit that Christianity itself.

> We can criticize the south Georgia Baptist church which
> excluded Clarence Jordan of Koinonia Farm from its
> membership. But . . . it was that same church which
> produced him in the first place.[24]

While Campbell recognized the role of the institutional church in these two examples, he remains suspicious of the churches' efforts to represent Christian teaching authentically. Most of his criticism was directed toward the inactivity of the churches. However, Campbell directed a strong measure of criticism toward one particular activity: the reliance of the mainline churches on formal education. For Campbell, himself a product of theological education, the church's reliance on education represented the

---

[24]"The Role of Religion in the Desegregation Controversy," 189- 190, 13-14. Campbell adds: "I have trouble when I'm talking about the institutional church, when you get to the black church. . . . I know that just as much corruption is there among the preachers." Campbell, second interview with author.

influence of modern culture on the institutional church. It had nothing to do with whether the churches embodied the ethics of the New Testament. Campbell's criticism of theological education was not of its role as a promoter of independent thought and intellectual. He believed that the churches equated theological education with authentic Christianity, and it was this aspect that he opposed.

Campbell believed that Christianity is relational rather than theological. That is, Campbell contended that the essence of Christianity had more to do with how a person lives than what a person believes. However, this belief that the essence of Christianity is relational does not serve the self-perpetuating needs of the institutional church. For this reason, Campbell thought that the institutional church developed its creedal systems. According to Campbell, "You can't build a steeple on an unconditional message. . . . There must be a club. Something to hold over their heads."[25] Organized religious thought—Campbell's definition of theology— was responsible for much of the violence throughout human history.

> The main thing that makes me fearful of theology, and thus theological preaching, is that theology so often leads to violence. Nothing is so dangerous as religion when it gets out of hand. . . . Too often we use a theology designed for slingshots and spears and apply it to a nuclear age.[26]

Campbell views the American divinity school or seminary as institutional Christianity's clearest failure. He holds that most American divinity schools reflect the culture of higher education, rather than a distinctive Christian worldview. "We assumed that if we had an enlightened and educated clergy," the institutional church would be closer to the ideals of the primitive Church than it was without an educated ministry. Campbell believes this

---

[25]*Forty Acres and a Goat*, 155.
[26]"Values and Hazards of Theological Preaching," 76.

assumption confused cultural sophistication with authentic Christianity. Moreover, cultural sophistication did not necessarily improve the churches and it often hampered them. While almost all churches required a professionally-trained clergy, Campbell said, "I will defy anyone to prove to me that the church today is more nearly the church of the first century; it's less."[27]

On the other hand, Campbell does not laud an illiterate ministry. Where the institutional churches need an understanding of authentic Christianity, theological education typically provides only cultural improvement.[28] The institutional churches, however, confuse cultural sophistication with authentic Christianity. Not only are two not synonymous; they are often antithetical. Institutions of higher education do not differ from any other institution, having their own agenda and standards. A speech to an assembly at the Southern Baptist Theological Seminary suggested how theological institutions are more shaped by the culture of higher education than that of the authentic Church. He informed the audience that he once asked a member of the Ku Klux Klan to join an academic procession at a divinity school, claiming that his robe would be no different from those of the professors. The Klansman responded that his robe would be different because it had a cross on it. He then explained the significance of the story:

> [I]t raises certain questions about the manner in which we have intellectualized the Gospel, theologized it, complicated it with the trappings of academe to make it intellectually respectable in the company of the learned [instead of] letting it remain the scandal.[29]

Campbell sees his views as neither anti-intellectual nor dishonest. He freely admits his participation in theological

---

[27]Caudill interview, 27.
[28]*Ibid.*
[29]Chapel Address at Southern Baptist Theological Seminary, Sound Recording.

education and the value of higher education in making a person more productive in society. "I've participated in the academic community at every level [and] encouraged my children to do the same thing."[30] But Campbell does not encourage anyone to see formal theological education as inherently Christian. He believed that the institutional churches had made education "a religion itself, as totalitarian as the other idols" of the culture. Moreover, Campbell believed that despite the strong educational standards of theological education, "the academy has not found a way to lose itself in the ghetto, black ghetto and white ghetto."[31]

Campbell's claim of a tension between the culture of higher education and the authentic Church was one of perspective. He wanted the churches to realize that all "wisdom does not come from class notes."[32] He said, "[I]t's such an arrogance to assume that that's the only place [theological education] that we can learn." Campbell admitted that "we can learn theology in a course of systematic theology or from scholarly journals that we read footnoted in journals. That is one place to learn theology, but it's not the only place."[33]

Campbell's Non-Institutional Understanding of the Church

The idea of the Church remained important, even vital, for Campbell's religious and social world view. His new ecclesiology saw the Church as present wherever christocentric ethics were practiced. The institutional church failed in its mission and ceased to be the Church, but the Church had not ceased to exist. According to Campbell, the Church "first of all must be the redeemed

---

[30]Dibble interview, 165.

[31]"The Computer Says 'Repent' (A Fable)," *Faith and Mission* 2 (Fall 1984):79, 80.

[32]*Forty Acres and a Goat*, 190.

[33]Dibble interview, 165.

community. Then it will be empowered to redeem the world, and not before."[34]

A redeemed community, as Campbell understood the concept, existed when people engaged in ethical actions. Since the actions of the institutional church were not always ethical, then the institution was not always the Church. The degree to which an organization reflected the nature of the Church, according to Campbell, rested on that organization's record of ethical action. This understanding of the Church was centered in actions. In *Forty Acres and a Goat*, an example of Campbell's mature thought, he paraphrased the doctrine of the Church held by Carlyle Marney, another progressive Southern Baptist who often said, "Church is a verb.[35]

Campbell thus believes that the work of the Church is often done by those who do not formally acknowledge the Christian faith. "I see others with no claim to being Christian" doing the work of the Church.[36] One of Campbell's most graphic illustrations of this idea came in his speech to the Conference on Race and Religion in 1963. Campbell told the audience about regularly patronizing a small grocery in front of his Nashville office when he was with the NCC. The grocery store was managed by an African American woman, but the building was owned by whites. The white owners used the other parts of the building to run a prostitution ring. The manager of the grocery died unexpectedly one day, which Campbell discovered when he entered the business and found the white owner of the property weeping. The incident occurred during a time when African Americans were attempting to attend white churches as part of the integration effort. Campbell saw "tragedy" and irony in the fact that the deceased African American woman would have been denied a chance to attend the area's white churches, while at the same time her death was mourned by the owner of a house of prostitution.

---

[34]*Race and the Renewal of the Church*, 4.
[35]*Forty Acres and a Goat*, 148.
[36]"A Man Had Two Sons," 37.

No wonder a prophet [Jesus] whom most white council members and most neighborhood association members call Lord said to some of the "good" people of his day that those who sold their bodies for pay . . . were closer to the Kingdom of which he spoke than they—"Truly I say to you, scalawags and whores enter the kingdom of God before you." Woe unto a generation when a human soul finds more acceptance and community in a whore house than in a church house![37]

Campbell's definition of the Church rested on the actions committed by the group, rather than on the group's claims of being a church. Thus for Campbell the institutional church of the 1960s, particularly the white churches in the South, failed to be the authentic Church described in the New Testament. Among whites, the Church existed only in the actions of those who challenged the segregation within the churches. Because many of these people left the South eventually, the Church was becoming nonexistent in the region. Quoting Leslie Dunbar of the Southern Regional Council, Campbell said, "[I]t has been these men [people] who have been, in any valid sense, the Church in the South these past few years." The teachings of Christ were often embodied in the work of those outside formal structures and many ministers left the institutional church, not because they had lost faith in their sense of being a minister, but because they felt unable to perform the ministry according to their belief systems.[38] This sense of Church and ministry is precisely the view that Campbell holds. He saw himself as "a Baptist preacher with no parish save forty acres and a goat."[39] By withdrawing from the institutional church, Campbell believes that he is being faithful to the authentic Church. What happens in the institutional churches on Sunday morning is not "the only expression of the beloved community."

---

[37]"The Inner Life of Church and Synagogue," 21-22.
[38]"Rumblings of Rebellion Among Southern White Clergy," 128-129.
[39]*Forty Acres and a Goat*, 13.

In a sense it is tragic that Christians seem obliged to go outside the framework of the church to bear witness. Nevertheless, such a witness is valid and efforts to relate faith to secular action groups cannot be dismissed as outside the pale of Christian social action.[40]

The Church, then, is a fluid concept, according to Campbell. No one organization is identical with the Church, although many organizations may do the work of the Church. Moreover, the Church does not exist in these organizations, but in the individuals associated with them. The work that Campbell sees as the work of the Church does not lie in the comprehensive work of a bureaucracy, but in work done by individuals at the local level. According to Campbell, the Church's work "is happening at the local level. Only there does the Church exist at all."[41]

In Campbell's ecclesiology the Church exists in a variety of contexts at the local level. None of these contexts has exclusive claim to being the Church; thus Campbell avoids equating any one context as being his Church. The nature of the Church is relational, and relations cannot be embodied in an institution. The Church exists wherever there are "relationships, in community, interacting or whatever word you might want to use to describe human being to human being." In *Brother to a Dragonfly*, Campbell recorded the definition of the Church given to him by a friend as "one cat in one ditch and one nobody son of a bitch trying to pull him out."[42]

When pressed to describe how he has experienced the Church personally, Campbell typically speaks of the people with whom he relates on a daily basis. He is also careful that he does not merely replace the structure of the institutional church with another structure that is less conventional. He has tried to be consistent in his definition. Asked about his relationship with the Church since

---

[40]*Race and the Renewal of the Church*, 73.
[41]"Rumblings of Rebellion Among the Southern White Clergy," 127.
[42]*Ibid.*; *Brother to a Dragonfly*, 177.

distancing himself from institutional religion, Campbell mentioned that he conducts funerals and weddings and visits people in the hospital. Frequently, these are people who live in his neighborhood or who are in the country music industry. According to Campbell, "that's going to Church."[43]

For Campbell, the Church exists in these positive relationships that he has cultivated with his friends and neighbors.

> How many people do you know that you can find at three in the morning . . . and they'd be there? So it's dangerous for more than one reason to say that's my Church. But if I understand the meaning of Church, that is my Church.[44]

The Church exists in relationships, and it happens for Campbell that many of these relationships have been formed in a Tennessee tavern. The tavern is incidental to the Church, though. "There's nothing sacred about a beer joint," Campbell said, "and there's nothing sacred in my judgment about the First Baptist Church."[45] While the tavern is not sacred, the people and their relationships are.

> I would not say, "The Church to me is Gass's Tavern." Never. Because pretty soon I would be writing essays that said find your local tavern and you've found the Church. I don't believe that. Pretty soon we'd be arguing about whether communion is a Coor's Beer or Black Jack Daniel's or whether it's a hamburger or a soda cracker. We'd just be starting it all over again.[46]

---

[43]Second interview by author.
[44]Dibble interview, 163.
[45]*Ibid.*
[46]Second interview by author.

Because of his relational, non-institutional ecclesiology, Campbell resists every effort to institutionalize his understanding of the Church. He has had numerous opportunities to do so, however. Richard Morrisoe, a priest wounded in the gunfire that killed Jonathan Daniels, held Mass on Campbell's property during his recovery. Many of Campbell's friends encourage him to make it a regular occurrence. Campbell does not believe that they could structurally create the Church, so he resisted. "To do that," Campbell responded, "is to start another institution," not the Church.[47] Campbell said that he found those efforts "offensive to my Anabaptist genes."[48]

Yet, Campbell believed that the work of the Church had often occurred on his forty acre farm near Nashville, Tennessee. On his land he has conducted baptisms, funerals, and weddings, all of which he calls "sacramental acts."[49] Campbell affirms the place of worship in the Church, but his understanding of worship is as non-institutional as his understanding of the Church. A person shows gratitude to God through "praise and song, in sacramental acts, [and] in worship."[50] All of these actions continued to have a place in Campbell's life despite his departure from the institutional church.

What Campbell had developed was a non-institutional understanding of the Church. In keeping with this expression, Campbell and several others assembled to ordain Andrew Lipscomb to the ministry. They did not do this to create a new denomination, however. Lipscomb, a United Methodist minister, was about to lose his ordination credentials because he would not accept a regular assignment by the denominational hierarchy. Calling themselves the Lazer Creek Congregation, the group ordained Lipscomb so he could continue to perform marriages and other duties. On another occasion, the group ordained a person

---

[47]Caudill interview, 92.
[48]*Forty Acres and a Goat*, 122.
[49]Dibble interview, 148.
[50]"What Do We Do About What Has Been Done?" Sound recording.

who performed several ministerial duties so that the person could be exempt from the military. A third person was ordained because she was unable to work with prisoners on death row without ministerial orders.

Campbell has also conducted baptisms on his property, including that of his grandson. He approached baptism as a sacrament that affirmed the positive status between humans and God as humans understand God. Campbell also baptized people in an effort to see that the institutional church was not the only place where sacraments were performed. Part of Campbell's liturgy included the words, "In violation of the steeples and Mr. Caesar [the government]." One such baptism provided Campbell an opportunity to reflect on his relationship to the authentic Church. He noted:

It was the most baptistic I had felt in a long time. Trouble-maker. Rebel. The left wing of the Reformation. That's what we once were. But that was a long time ago.[51]

Campbell also regularly performed marriages as part of the work of the Church. Again, his practice of this function illustrated his non-institutional understanding of the Church. He was once asked by an aspiring member of a local country music band to perform a wedding at a local bar. Campbell at first resisted the idea because he felt that the act would be reduced to a mockery. He did not want to perform the ceremony simply as part of a "nightclub act." The young groom provided Campbell with additional details, however, that persuaded Campbell. The ceremony was to take place only in the presence of friends and family after the club had closed for the night. What the groom "was saying was, 'this is my Church and those are my people.' So it [the wedding] was at the Exit Inn in Nashville."[52]

---

[51]*Forty Acres and a Goat*, 153-154, 158, 168-169.
[52]Second interview with author.

Campbell believes that what occurs under the aegis of the institutional churches rarely constitutes the authentic Church. When he spoke to a group of United Methodist ministers in 1986 at Emory University, he called on those present to engage in a massive reform of their churches. The proposed reforms included: increasing the number of female bishops, opening the churches to the homeless, requiring that ten percent of all corporate donations to church affiliated colleges be used for poverty relief, and the payment of taxes by the churches. He then listed a final, more likely option: "We can walk away sorrowfully, for behold, . . . we are very rich."[53] Campbell thus implied that the mainline churches had greater difficulty exhibiting authentic Christianity than other forces in society.

Sectarian Christianity, however, did provide Campbell with an appropriate paradigm. The paradigm of the sects has value for Campbell not only because of its symbolic value but also because Campbell believes that the sects had actually come closer to authentic Christianity than any other institution, especially in the area of race relations. Campbell has made this point in several ways since the 1960s. In *Race and the Renewal of the Church*, Campbell quoted a statement by a church leader that said, "[I]t is sinful to have two congregations in the same community for persons of separate and distinct races." After quoting this statement, Campbell suggested that most readers would assume that the words belonged to a resolution of a progressive, mainline denomination. These words, however, did not come from the mainline churches. Rather, a Church of Christ minister, David Lipscomb, said them in 1878. The quotation served to argue that social activism occurred long before the mainline churches entered the arena. He did not necessarily endorse the record of the Church of Christ in race relations, since the school that bore Lipscomb's name was still segregated at the time Campbell wrote his book. However, Lipscomb, as a product of a sectarian environment, called for integration in the churches long before the issue was

---

[53]"What Do We Do About What Has Been Done?" Sound recording.

popular, and he did so motivated by "the life and teachings of Jesus Christ," rather than court orders and rulings.[54]

Campbell also saw the sectarian ideal embodied in the life of Horace Germany, a Mississippi Church of God minister without formal theological training. In 1959, Germany attempted to start the Bay Ridge Christian College in Neshoba County. The school was to have been an interracial institution for the training of Church of God ministers. When Germany refused to yield to threats and close the school, he was severely beaten and forced to move. Campbell's interest in the man was not solely one of compassion. Germany's sectarian worldview, which governed his thinking, appealed to Campbell. Germany did not integrate his school because of the Supreme Court ruling, but because "[t]he Gospel . . . is a universal Gospel to all men, as given by Christ in the Great Commission." Campbell believed that while the mainline churches received the greatest amount of publicity in race relations, the most active whites in the support of integration were the leaders of small, sectarian groups.[55]

Personal reasons also influenced Campbell's interest in the sects. When Campbell's younger brother, Paul, suffered a divorce, he was unable to find solace within a traditional church. Campbell said that the "split-level Baptists, now grown rich" offered his brother "nothing but a weekly appointment . . . with a young Th.D. probing his psyche." On the other hand,

> [T]he "holy rollers" could, and did, offer him a place where he could cry out to an empathizing audience who would cry with him because they loved him, a place where he could laugh out loud and shout God's goodness. . . .[56]

---

[54]*Race and the Renewal of the Church*, 29-31.

[55]*Brother to a Dragonfly*, 157; "Rumblings of Rebellion Among Southern White Clergy," 124-125.

[56]*Brother to a Dragonfly*, 42-43.

The most graphic sectarian image used by Campbell did not come from his brother's new denomination or from Campbell's experience in civil rights. For this part of his sectarian paradigm, Campbell turned to the snake handling sects of Tennessee. Snake handling developed in eastern Tennessee during the early 1900s, among believers who took literally Mark 16:18, a passage that promises the faithful that they can drink poison and handle poisonous snakes without harm. Biblical scholars of all traditions largely reject the authenticity of the passage, although it remains in many English translations. Because of the obvious dangers associated with the practice, as well as the fact that this sect draws its members from powerless members of society, many state legislatures in Appalachian states have banned its observance.[57]

During a trial in Tennessee for two Holiness Church of God ministers accused of violating a Tennessee law prohibiting the practice, Campbell visited the congregation and attended the court proceedings. One of the defenses expressed by the ministers was, "We live by the Bible." To be certain, this phrase was value-laden and the cause and embodiment of many "errors and misinterpretations." Yet, the phrase and its goal retained value. Mainline Christianity, by rejecting sectarianism and biblicism for dominant cultural values, was no better than the groups that retained biblicism. Perhaps, Campbell argued, the sectarian groups were superior because they attempted to keep a biblically-centered faith, even if their hermeneutic was faulty.

The symbolism of snake handling provided Campbell with even more insight into the nature of the authentic Church. According to Campbell, these radical Pentecostals do not handle snakes out of reverence, but to demonstrate that they have overcome "the evil which they represent." Snakes represent evil and danger, and the snake-handling Christians lift them up to demonstrate their faith and deliverance from evil. Mainline, institutional churches, have their serpents, but the evil snakes are the "reptilic idols of civilization" or cultural values. However, the institutional churches do not

---

[57]*Dictionary of Christianity in America*, s.v. "Snake Handling," by Daniel Reid.

"lift up" their serpents or cultural values to conquer their evil. Rather, "[t]he rationale of the institutional steeple for lifting up the serpents of culture is that they are sacred." The mainline church has embraced the culture, rather than challenged it. Campbell did not advocate that people adopt snake handling Pentecostalism in order to become the authentic Church, but the group did provide him a sectarian image by which to measure the institutional churches. He affirms that

> despite some occasional unpleasant side effects from handling copperheads and drinking strychnine, when placed alongside the side effects . . . brought into Appalachia by . . . the mainline, steepled, structured institutions . . . equating the Christian faith with civilization . . . then the handling of live reptiles looks pretty harmless.[58]

The Novel as a Forum for Campbell's Thought

From 1982 to 1988, Campbell wrote three novels that explore his understanding of true religion. Although he discussed that theme in several of his essays and his nonfiction books, his works of historical fiction provide the strongest expression of his religious thought. Utilizing groups such as the Anabaptists, poor Southerners, and the Southern Baptist Convention, Campbell used the method of historical fiction to present his message.

While each book has a different setting, certain themes appear in each of the books that link them together. Each novel uses fictional characters, some of which are based on real individuals, to express his understanding of religion. The books grow out of the thought of the mature Campbell, a man in his sixties when he wrote the books. Each book uses ideas from Anabaptist and Baptist history to illustrate his understanding of religion. Campbell first became exposed to Anabaptist thought while a student at Yale

---

[58]"Which is the Real Evil–Snake-Handling or the Establishment Church?" *Southern Voices*, March-April 1974, 46-48.

Divinity School under church historian Roland Bainton. The Anabaptists, according to Campbell, "really did believe something." Campbell was especially appreciative of the role of Anabaptists in the struggle for religious liberty.[59]

The books do not advocate the embrace of every aspect of institutional Baptist structures. Indeed, the books selectively embrace certain portions of Anabaptist and Baptist history to the exclusion of other portions. What Campbell presents is an idealized account of sectarian religion, and the ideal, glorified in his stories, represents authentic Christianity. The Anabaptist and Baptist heritages suggest what it means (and what it does not mean) to practice Christianity in the twentieth century.

Campbell wrote *The Glad River* in 1982, and at times has considered it the best of his books, as well as "the most original writing" that he had done.[60] His first major venture into the world of fictional writing, *The Glad River* tells the story of three southern men who became friends during their World War II military service. Claudy Momber, known as Doops, is a white Mississippi native from the imaginary city of Claughton Station. Kingston Smylie is the illegitimate son of a poor girl from an ethnic minority group and a well-off, but irascible young man. When the father abandoned the expectant mother, the paternal grandfather adopted the mother, moved to another fictional Mississippi community, and reared the young Smylie as his own son. The mother and grandfather present themselves to the public and to the son as husband and wife. On Smylie's sixteenth birthday, the grandfather who had acted as father tells the young man the whole story. The third major character, Fordache Arceneau, is a Cajun from south Louisiana.

The book has a simple, straightforward story line. The three men meet shortly after being drafted, go through basic training, and serve together in the Pacific theater. Doops's superiors order

---

[59]Ibid.
[60]Second interview by author.

him to capture a Japanese soldier hiding in the jungle, which he successfully does. In spite of the official hostility between the captor and his prisoner, the two men form a friendship that cuts across language, citizenship, politics, and religion. On their journey back to the base, the prisoner became miserably ill with some jungle malady. Eventually, the diseased prisoner begs Doops to kill him and end his misery, and Doops carries out this final request. As a result of the trauma, Doops suffers a nervous breakdown, but recovers to return to a normal life in the United States.

The three wartime buddies continue their friendship in America, but tragedy soon strikes the group. Arceneau, who acquired the nickname Model T in the service, stands accused of raping and murdering his girlfriend who rejected him. The defense decides to call Arceneau as a witness, but his refusal to take an oath on religious grounds further incriminates him. After Arceneau is executed, Doops and Smylie steal his body and secretly bury it deep in a Louisiana marsh.

Throughout the simple narrative, Campbell weaves a story about Doops's personal religious pilgrimage. Doops's mother wants him to get baptized, but he refuses, choosing instead to be baptized by Arceneau shortly before Arceneau's execution. The book explores another religious theme through Doops's mental breakdown. In his hospital room, the ailing Doops begins writing a story about Anabaptists in Holland. Asked by his nurse what he is doing, he answers, "It's about how there aren't any Baptists left in the world."[61] In Campbell's original draft of *The Glad River* he has the character Doops reading large portions of the book about Anabaptists. Much of this material was deleted by Campbell's editor. One year after the publication of *The Glad River* Campbell gathered the deleted material and compiled it into a separate book.

Containing eighty-three pages that were originally a part of *The Glad River*, this material was expanded into a novella called,

---

[61]Ibid., 136.

Cecelia's Sin.[62] The introduction, written by Eric Gritsch, gives an overview of the Anabaptist movement to set the context for the book's fictionalized account. Campbell admired Gritsch as one the church historians in the United States who specialized in Anabaptist studies.[63] The remaining chapters add detail to the imaginary story told by Doops in Campbell's first novel. The book treats the story of Cecelia Geronymus, Goris Cooman, and Pieter Boens. The three Anabaptists fear that they have been betrayed to the authorities as members of this illegal sect. As they await their arrest, Cecelia, like Doops, decides to write the story of the Anabaptists.

Searching for the key idea of the movement, Cecelia settles on the Anabaptist idea of community of goods as the fundamental teaching of the movement. Community of goods, and the sense of community accompanying it, has caused the persecution against their movement because it undercuts the power of the state. After discussing community and other Anabaptist doctrines, the three fugitives are arrested and taken to certain martyrdom.[64] *Cecelia's Sin* is loosely based on *The Mennonite Encyclopedia* and *Martyrs Mirror*. However, the book is not simply a tale about religious persecution in Holland during the Reformation; it also conveys Campbell's assessment of modern religion. The historical setting of the Radical Reformation provides Campbell a platform in the past to address the present.

Campbell's *The Convention* moves from commenting on wartime friendship and Dutch Anabaptism to a parody of the schism that started in the Southern Baptist Convention in 1979. Just as *The Glad River* is only ostensibly about wartime friends, and *Cecelia's Sin* is only partially about Anabaptist martyrdom, *The Convention* gives more than a fictionalized account about conflict in a large, conservative denomination. This 1988 novel uses the events

---

[62]Second interview by author.
[63]"On Silencing Our Finest," *Christianity and Crisis*, 16 September 1985, 341.
[64]*Cecelia's Sin* (Macon, Georgia: Mercer University Press, 1983), 34, 80-82.

connected with a successful effort to change the leadership in the Southern Baptist Convention to present Campbell's ecclesiology.

Campbell wrote the book in light of the shift in the Southern Baptist Convention toward rigid fundamentalism. He saw this shift as a further deterioration of the nexus between modern Baptists and the Anabaptists of the 1500s.

> I knew that there was something historically that the Baptist movement had [and lost]. I don't know of another movement in history, where the Christian movement is concerned, that is more important than the Anabaptists.[65]

Campbell's use of the Southern Baptist Convention as a model to discuss ecclesiology is not an endorsement of the Moderate, anti-Fundamentalist party, however. Although his sympathies lie more with the Moderates who lost control of the SBC, Campbell assessed the Moderate institutional structure as inherently self-serving. In describing the two factions in Southern Baptist life, Campbell called the differences a choice between "the conservatives or the slightly more conservative."[66] In Campbell's assessment, as an institution the Southern Baptist Convention departed from authentic Christianity "long before the Fundamentalists took over."[67]

The story concerns an innocent couple who represent their small, rural church at the national convention of the Federal Baptist Church. Dorcas and Excell McBride arrive at the convention only to find a host of auxiliary groups competing for loyalty. By some strange chance, the women's caucus drafts Dorcas to run for president of the convention as their candidate, opposing both the fundamentalist candidate and the candidate backed by the old denominational bureaucracy.[68]

---

[65]Second interview by author.
[66]"On Silencing Our Finest," 341.
[67]Second interview by author.
[68]*The Convention* (Atlanta: Peachtree, 1988), 54, 193, passim.

When Dorcas scores an upset victory, she shocks all the involved parties by promptly resigning. The book opens with Dorcas answering the question, "What is the Church?" with her statement that "the Church is where people love one another."[69] The narrative of the book contrasts the definition of Dorcas with the reality of the denominational structure. The group that claims to be the church is far from her definition. Although she resigns her position at the end of the book, Dorcas does not change her definition of the Church. She has decided that the true church (or true religion) and institutional religion are two different, mutually exclusive things. As with his other novels, Campbell has chosen a particular context in religious history to serve as a setting for expressing his own thought about religion.

Will Campbell has spent much of his energy expressing the view that institutional religion and its trappings are quite different from religion as practiced by individuals. The persecuted Anabaptists provide a model of authentic religion, according to Campbell, especially when contrasted with modern religion. Many early Baptists and Anabaptists believed in the separation of church and state, supported pacifism, opposed the death penalty, refused to take oaths or participate in the government, and argued that every human had a free conscience. The political and ecclesiastical powers of the 1500s persecuted the Anabaptists for holding these nonconformist views. One fact illustrates the decline of the modern church as Campbell understands it. Most modern Baptists reject these religious views. For Campbell, that rejection is a denial of their heritage.[70] But is it a denial of their heritage? While the ethical issues lauded by Campbell undoubtedly have a prominent place in Anabaptist history, they have never been a part of modern Baptist life. The Baptist tradition that has been dominant in America owes a greater direct debt to those English Baptists who emerged out of Separatism. While a sectarian group with a strong

---

[69]Ibid., 6.
[70]Ibid., 38.

tradition of advocating religious liberty, these Baptists were not as radical as the continental Anabaptists. Campbell, however, is less concerned with providing an historical study of Baptist origins than he is with holding up the Anabaptist tradition as an ideal for the modern churches to emulate.

What is the essence of true religion? What is the single idea that gives rise to these ethical ideas? Campbell argues that community is the essence of true religion. He equates community with the true church and contrasted community with institutional religion. At the end of *The Convention*, a character again comments on the church. Just as Dorcas earlier defined the church as a place where people love each other, so now at the close of the story Dorcas expresses the church in purely non-institutional terms. One of Dorcas's foster children, Leanne, gives the evening prayer.

> Leanne prayed the way she always did, for everything and everybody. . . . Then Leanne called the names of everyone in the family and all the neighbors she could remember—especially for "Mister Leland who lives in the tar paper house on the left, just before you cross the river on the way to town who is bad sick. . . . She thanked God for bringing Mama and Daddy home safely. She prayed for the fireflies in the jar and promised God that she would turn them loose in the morning if they didn't smother.

After this long, child-like prayer, another child commented to Dorcas that "Leanne forgot to pray for the church." Dorcas responds, "No she didn't," the last words of the book.[71] Campbell did not use the characters to say that religion is unimportant or that true religion is never put into practice. Rather, Campbell ended the book by showing what he believes true religion is: faith practiced in highly individual terms with little regard for any traditional structures. The Church is not where the sacraments are

---

[71]Ibid., 406.

practiced or where dogma is proclaimed, but "where people love one another."

Cecelia's Sin expresses this same anti-institutional understanding of the Church. Cecelia asks the other two fugitive Anabaptists to name the one thing that has brought both Church and State to oppose them. The state opposed their pacifism and their ban on oath-taking. The civil authorities especially opposed their idea of believers' baptism because infant baptism provided the state a population count. Campbell's observations about the state do not reflect an anti-government conviction. They reflect his belief that all institutions are self-serving, a belief from which he does not exclude government. None of these things, according to the story, constitutes the basic problem. The powers in control opposed the Anabaptists mainly because of the sect's concept of community.

Responding to Cecelia's question, Pieter answers that "community of goods" is the thing most disconcerting to the opponents of the Anabaptists. According to Campbell's idea of Anabaptist community, the community was rooted in mutual love, not doctrine. Mutual love, however, does not provide the control that authority provides. For this reason, community, which is the basis of mutual love, "is what they fear most. It is community which they fear will be their undoing."[72]

What is community of goods? Two types of community of goods existed among the Anabaptists. Most Anabaptists practiced a general form of communal sharing. The Hutterites practiced a more "radical community of love" that entailed primitive communism. According to one Hutterite, "If Christian love to the neighbor cannot achieve as much community in things temporal [as in things spiritual], in assistance and counsel, then the blood of Christ does not cleanse a man from his sins."[73]

---

[72]*Cecelia's Sin*, 34.

[73]Harold S. Bender. *The Mennonite Encyclopedia: A Comprehensive Reference Work on the Anabaptist-Mennonite Movement* (Hillsboro, Kansas: Mennonite Brethren Publishing House, 1955-1959), s.v. "Community of Goods," by R. Foth.

Most Anabaptists practiced the less rigid concept of community that is more an expression of mutual love than true primitive communism. The political authorities attempted to link the Hutterites' economic practices with the practices of all Anabaptists. Mainstream Anabaptists, such as Menno Simons, made every attempt to distinguish their more general concept of communal charity from the radical common ownership practiced by the Hutterites.[74] Campbell's character, Pieter, is historically accurate when he distinguishes between Hutterite communism and the more general sharing of community. "[Communal ownership] is not our practice here. . . . We do not urge one another to sell our property. We have no common treasury."[75] The Anabaptists were at their best, according to Campbell, when they practiced community as natural sharing, not as a systematic plan.

In choosing community as the fundamental concept of the Anabaptist movement, Campbell used keen insight. Indeed, many of the Anabaptist doctrines logically relate to community or sharing. Discipleship especially relates to a concept of community. A person "is but a steward of . . . worldly possessions, which he must be ready to share at any time with others," according to one understanding of community.

Many of the Anabaptist leaders stressed community in their writings. Balthasar Hubmaier said "that a man should have a concern for the other man, that the hungry be fed, the thirsty receive drink, etc., for we are not the masters of our possessions but stewards and distributors only."[76] Menno Simons defended the Anabaptist concept of community as general sharing against those opponents who wanted to connect all Anabaptists with more radical strains. Community did not require the systematic attempts of the Hutterites.

---

[74]Menno Simons, *The Complete Writings of Menno Simons*, corrected ed., trans.. Leonard Verduin and ed. J. C. Wenger, with a biography by Harold S. Bender (Scottdale, Pennsylvania: Herald Press, 1956), 558.

[75]*Cecelia's Sin*, 34.

[76]Bender, *The Mennonite Encyclopedia*, s.v. "Community of Goods."

In fact, Menno Simons saw community as a natural product of true Christian living. When a practicing Christian cares for another person, the Christian will instinctively work for "the welfare of the other." Calculated programs of sharing and communal ownership should not be necessary. The practicing Christian needs no organized economic system to induce sharing and community. The Church as a community is like the human body, according to Menno Simons. When a part of the body is unclothed or in need, one does not need a systematic plan to address the need. The person automatically responds to the need in an instinctive manner. Likewise, so "it should be with those who are the Lord's Church and body." The sense of community described by Simons naturally happens, he believed, when true religion is practiced. Community was a critical mark of his concept of true Christianity. If members of the Church did not automatically care for one another without the aid of some system, then people "may well abandon the whole Gospel of our Lord Jesus Christ."[77]

The Glad River articulates this sense of automatic, instinctive community. Just as Pieter in *Cecelia's Sin* distinguished between the programmed community of the Hutterites and the concept of community based on general voluntary sharing held by Simons, Doops discusses community in *The Glad River*. Community is not something that human effort can create, nor is it a doctrine to be contemplated. Doops defines community as "a bunch of folks getting along for some reason. . . . It just happens. We don't make it. We don't make community any more than we make souls. It's created."[78] With Doops's statements, Campbell expressed what he believed is positive about the Christian religion: its power to move people to do good. Christianity in its authentic expression will make people automatically come together in community.

Campbell's Dorcas McBride provides an example of the actions of one committed to community. At the meeting of the women's organization at the Federal Baptist Convention, Dorcas listened to

---

[77]Menno, 558-559.
[78]*The Glad River*, 59.

the main speaker call on the women to take "over contemporary structures so women would not continue to be closed out of power politics." For Campbell, such posturing has little to do with religion and more to do with power. The corporate structures will be as fundamentally corrupt with women in control as the same structures have been with male dominance. That the speaker is talking about power reveals Campbell's fear that all humans can become enslaved to a particular agenda. When Dorcas heard the speaker, she questioned the topic's relevance for the average person back in her rural community. Dorcas announced that she was not as concerned about empowerment and other ideological views as she was about aiding the poor, helping the sick, feeding the hungry, and visiting prisoners.[79] Dorcas did not do these things out of any plan to reconstruct society. She did them naturally because they were the right things to do.

Community is not about proper structures or correctly defined doctrines. When Arceneau asks Doops why he and his mother fight about religion, Doops answers, "That's what religion is. . . . A man's religion is what he'll get mad enough to fight about." Institutional religion is not about God, according to Campbell, but about humans competing with one another.[80] The Church as an institution with an agenda stands in a different spectrum than that of true community. Institutional religion is concerned with power. Community, which is rooted in discipleship, concerns itself with action.

> Only discipleship is real. We can follow what little we know of God. And we know enough to follow. Enough to get us in trouble. Discipleship leads to our cross. Doctrine leads to concentration camps for those who do not agree.[81]

---

[79]*The Convention*, 68, 69.
[80]*The Glad River*, 189-190.
[81]*The Convention*, 382-383.

Campbell used the Anabaptists as models to criticize an ideological approach to faith. Community occurs as a gift from the divine, he might say. When humans attempt to build institutions on the basis of the original community, they inevitably become caretakers of a particular system. Hence Campbell contrasted discipleship with doctrine. He also contrasted the experience of his three imaginary Anabaptists with the violent Anabaptist-inspired revolt in Münster. The early Anabaptists, even the mainstream Anabaptists that Campbell contrasts with the revolutionaries, were more active in building a community than were Campbell's fictional characters. The historical Anabaptists believed that they had recovered the New Testament community, and that their actions were creating this community.

In the northern European town of Münster economic and social unrest combined with political change to create an especially volatile situation. From 1533 to 1535, radical Anabaptists gained control of the city and started a new political order. They based the new order on apocalyptic imagery, hoping to bring in a restoration of the Old Testament theocracy. These particularly radical Anabaptists hoped to bring in a millennial kingdom through their actions.

Bernard Rothmann was one of the extremist leaders. Born in Münster in 1495, he served as a minister at St. Maurice in the city for one year, left for advanced study, and returned to preach increasingly Protestant sermons. In 1532, Rothmann sympathizers on the city council forced the Roman Catholic priests out of their positions, placing the city and the church structures in decidedly Lutheran hands. The Lutheran phase lasted only about one year. Rothmann became more radical in his theology, adopting believers' baptism and eventually gaining political control of the town. Rothmann's success in gaining followers came to the attention of Jan Mathijs and John Beukels, as well as to other followers of Melchior Hoffman. When Beukels and Mathijs arrived in the town, they undertook a revolutionary restructuring of the social order. The two men trained the citizens for an armed revolt, introduced communism, and merged the Church and State. Not only did these radicals hold property in common, they also held their marriages in common with the introduction of polygamy.

Rothmann's experiment reached its climax with his period of restorationism. Based on Acts 3: 21, the restitution of primitive religion as Rothmann understood it viewed human history as a set of "falls and restorations," starting with the Creation story and the Exodus, and moving to his contemporary situation with the perceived lack of forward vision of the magisterial reformers.[82] With bizarre history and selective choices of scripture as a guide, Rothmann rejected any notion of waiting on the Lord. He believed that he had discovered the pattern to usher in a new era for religion and humanity. His efforts failed miserably. Eventually, opposing troops reclaimed the city, ending Rothmann's social and religious experiment, as well as his life.

The Münster disaster provided a perfect historical model for Campbell to make his point that human reform efforts, especially those efforts inspired by religion, are in vain. As Cecelia writes an account of the movement, she interviews a young man from Münster who did not follow Rothmann. The followers of Rothmann were not true Anabaptists because they attempted to create community, even resorting to violence in their efforts. The Münsterites according to *Cecelia's Sin*, were "Lutherans [who] got halfway converted by some Anabaptists." After these "halfway Anabaptists" lost in their effort to hold on to political power, the "real Lutherans" placed blame for the entire rebellion on the those people Campbell calls real Anabaptists. However, had the Münsterites succeeded, Campbell wrote that "the persecution of the Anabaptists would have gone on just the same."[83] He implied that whoever holds the power will necessarily oppose those out of power. *The Glad River* articulates this idea in a scene that describes a trainload of Japanese-Americans heading to a relocation center. Doops, Kingston, and Arceneau are ordered to watch the train pass

---

[82]George Hunston Williams, *The Radical Reformation* (Philadelphia: Westminster Press, 1962), 364-377.

[83]*Cecelia's Sin*, 39.

through as part of their basic training. When the train stops, Doops noticed a Japanese girl momentarily leaving the train to remove the garbage. "Even the persecuted persecute," Campbell says through Doops's character.[84]

In his novels Campbell contrasts the institutional church with the true church represented by community. Just as one of Dorcas's children asks for a definition of the Church, one of the Anabaptists in *Cecelia's Sin* asks, "Where's the church?" Cecelia has the opportunity to express for Campbell an understanding of true community and true faith. She says that "the Church is here," pointing around the room at her three friends. Alluding to the teachings of Christ, she says that the Church is "where two or three are gathered." Goris responds by asking, "What about four or five?" Goris then comments on his rhetorical question. He says:

> I think two or three. But not four or five. . . . Because when there are more than two or three they start looking for a leader. He's in the midst of two or three but not four or five or eight hundred.[85]

Dealing with the same theme in *The Glad River*, Kingston asks for "the difference between a community and country." Doops responds, much in the same way as the previously mentioned passage in *Cecelia's Sin*. The mark distinguishing a community from a country (by implication, an organized institution) is structure and organization. In a community, the followers are all equal. All communities will lose the original vision as the subsequent generations attempt to define it and preserve it on their own terms. According to Campbell, the community cannot be preserved through structures. Community is a divine gift. As structure develops, leadership emerges, with "somebody [who] wants to

---

[84]*The Glad River*, 27.
[85]Ibid., 72-73.

improve on it, make it better because it gets bigger." When that process occurs, then there is "no more community."[86]

In a 1990 interview, Campbell expanded on his distinction between the institutional church and community. He defined the true Church in strictly non-institutional terms. He said, "Hell, I don't know what the Church is. Jesus said . . . that he was going to *build* the Church. . . . He didn't ask me to build it. And he certainly didn't ask me to define it." Campbell, however, made an effort in his novels to define the Church, as well as to critique the work of the institutional Church. His novels describe the true Church in terms of what it does, not in terms of what it thinks. Nor does he express the Church in terms of any lasting structure whatsoever. "The Church," Campbell said, "*is* at work in the world." What Campbell had less certainty about was a visible identity for the Church. While he affirmed a belief in a true Church, he also said that he did not "know what Jesus is up to or where His Church is."[87]

The three novels express this belief that the true Church is non-institutional. Campbell chose themes related to Baptist and Anabaptist history to make the contrast. His characters, at least the virtuous ones, are searching for Anabaptist, non-ideological ideals, expressed with the theme of community. In *The Convention*, Dorcas became Campbell's idea of a modern Anabaptist by rejecting the structured Church for the informal sense of Church as a place where people love one another. But how close is Campbell to the Anabaptist ideal when he dismisses the institutional Church?

Menno Simons, mentioned positively in *Cecelia's Sin*, understood the idea of community. However, he also had an understanding of the institutional Church as a legitimate religious category. While he called the Church "the community of God," he also specified the Church as "an assembly of the pious." In the same writing, Menno also gave signs or marks that identified the

---

[86]*The Glad River*, 60.
[87]McNabb interview, 13.

true Church. While some of these marks were ethical, such as mutual love, others were more tangible. For example, the true Church will follow the "salutary and unadulterated doctrine" of Jesus.[88] The Waterland Confession, a doctrinal standard written in 1580 by the heirs of Menno Simons, also had an institutional understanding of the Church.

"Believing and regenerated men, dispersed throughout the whole earth, are the true people of God or Church of Jesus Christ in the Earth," according to Article Twenty-Four. Article Twenty--Five gives insight into the nature of this Church as an institution. This passage calls for expulsion of those people holding membership who violate the teachings of the group. By the time the Mennonites adopt the definitive Dordrecht Confession, the Church is defined as a "visible Church of God," an institutional structure that consists not only of the baptized and the repentant, but of those who have "rightly *believed* [italics mine]."[89]

That Menno Simons understood the legitimacy of the institutional Church is reflected in his support of excommunication. Christians should "not have anything to do," he wrote in 1541, "with people who . . . [follow] false doctrine or a vain and carnal life." In 1558, Menno gave specific instructions on the ban or excommunication. Those people who join with the Church and then depart from the doctrinal or ethical teachings of the Church are to be expelled. If Menno did not have a well-defined concept of a gathered or institutional Church, then he would not have needed to rely on rigidly enforced standards. Since he defined the Church not only in spiritual terms, but also in terms of "a congregation of saints and an assembly of the righteous," Menno felt that those members who did not keep the standards subjected themselves to excommunication.[90] For the Anabaptists, community was

---

[88]Menno, 735, 738.

[89]"The Waterland Confession," in *Baptist Confessions of Faith*, ed. William Lumpkin (Philadelphia: Judson Press, 1959), 57-58; "The Dordrecht Confession," 71.

[90]Menno, 412, 965-967.

more than an elusive, hard-to-define concept. Menno and many of the other Anabaptists did not hold a non-institutional understanding of the Church. Rather, they had a well-defined concept of the nature and membership of the Church, a concept that involved doctrine as much as it involved discipleship and community.

Do the institutional characteristics of the Anabaptists invalidate Campbell's use of Anabaptist themes in his fiction? I do not think so. Campbell has not merely written about Anabaptists or wartime friendship or denominational schisms. Campbell used these ideas to express his understanding of true religion, as well as to express his belief that all institutions are inherently self-serving. He found in the Anabaptists a model that can be used to express not only his understanding of the left wing of the Reformation but also his understanding of contemporary religion. He is not writing history. He is using history. If his assessments are well-grounded, then he is using history well. However, it is likely that Campbell has utilized the Anabaptists of history in his effort to use them as a model for the present. He has not written a history of Anabaptists, although he has based his novel loosely on history.

The Critique of Contemporary Religion in Campbell's Novels

Campbell used the Anabaptist idea of community to express his understanding of the nature of authentic religion. As he discussed community, he made a contrast, both implicitly and explicitly, between the state of modern religion and modern society. The other issues Campbell addressed in these novels make a more obvious comment about his assessment of the role of religion.

As mentioned earlier, Campbell did not discuss every Anabaptist or Baptist distinctive in his books. He made no mention of the ban, the Anabaptist concept of an institutional Church, or the often rigidly orthodox theology of the Anabaptists. In fact, his de-emphasis of doctrine is not typical of much Anabaptist thought. Campbell selected certain Anabaptist doctrines to emphasize his own ecclesiology, but he neglected others. The Anabaptist doctrines chosen by Campbell uphold the autonomy of the individual. By discussing baptism, separation of Church and State, pacifism, and opposition to the death penalty, Campbell chose themes that protect the freedom of individuals from the power of any corporate entity.

In *Cecelia's Sin*, Campbell stressed the concept of believers' baptism. In discussing baptism, the characters develop their reasons for opposing infant baptism as much as they give their understanding of believers' baptism. When Cecelia asks her two companions why the authorities so oppose believers' baptism, the three do not discuss doctrinal ideas about conversion or original sin's effect on the infant. Rather, they discuss the use of infant baptism by the state to gain control over individuals. Campbell's story does not discuss infant baptism as much as it discusses the role of the state-established church in infant baptism. The state used infant baptism, according to Campbell, to gain control over its citizens. Merging religion and the civil order demands for the state a position of ultimate loyalty. The merger also claimed for the state ultimate authority.[91] Campbell's discussion of baptism in *Cecelia's Sin* deals less with the theology of baptism and more with the use of religious dogma by an institution to gain loyalty.

In writing *Cecelia's Sin*, Campbell used many sources to research the background and key ideas of his story, including *The Mennonite Encyclopedia*.[92] The article on baptism naturally discusses the theology of believers' baptism. However, the piece also discusses the relationship of the State to infant baptism. Infant baptism involves more than a perceived departure from the practices of the primitive Church. The baptism of infants served as a "necessary pillar of the state Church system." The state's use for baptism, according to the article, explains its interest in preserving what otherwise would be a simple doctrinal issue.[93] The article also gives insight into Campbell's interest in this particular doctrine. The

---

[91]*Cecelia's Sin*, 22-23.

[92]First interview by author, Phone call, Waco, Texas to Nashville, Tennessee, 15 May 1992.

[93]Bender, *The Mennonite Encyclopedia*, s.v. "Baptism," by Bender.

practice of believers' baptism challenged the authority of the state. By the time Doops questions the concept of baptism, the state no longer has an interest in baptism. The culture, especially the culture of the American South, does have an interest. Doops's chaplain summons him to the office to encourage him to be baptized. The chaplain wants Doops to be baptized so that Doops's mother will be happy and so that the chaplain can hire Doops as an assistant. He tells Doops that work in the chaplaincy will keep him out of combat. Baptism, or affiliation with a religion, while not an aspect of the state, seems to have many non-religious motives. Campbell rejects these motives.

Other Anabaptist doctrines emphasized by Campbell center on the value of life and the individual. These themes also hold authorities in a negative view. For example, the state executes Arceneau after his conviction for the murder of his girlfriend. Arceneau's refusal to take an oath contributed to his conviction.[94] The narrative not only picks up on the Anabaptist prohibition against oaths and the death penalty, it also reflects one of the reasons for opposition to these policies: opposition to ultimate state control.

In Campbell's choice of the Anabaptists as a model to express his own opposition to the all-encompassing civil institution, he remained faithful to the original reasons the early radicals opposed the oath and the death penalty. When the Anabaptists took stands against these practices on the basis of their understanding of certain scriptures, they came into conflict with the State. This encounter raised the issue of State-imposed policies that infringe on the individual conscience. Campbell is as suspicious of the state as an institution as he is of religious elements. His suspicion of government precedes his recovery of the Anabaptist heritage, and is probably more due to his experiences than to his theology. However, the discovery of Anabaptists as a sectarian tradition with which Campbell shared many views drew him to identify with that historical movement.

---

[94]*The Glad River*, 92, 230, 277-286.

Menno Simons complained about the large number of transactions that required an oath. His rigid understanding of scripture led him to think that "the Lord has so plainly forbidden the swearing of oaths to all Christians." He found it incredulous that an oath should be required since truthfulness should be a standard practice. Menno Simons's refusal to take an oath reflected far more than adherence to a sectarian rule. His belief involved questions of ultimate allegiance. Did the state have the right to force a person to engage in practices that violate personal convictions? Menno held that the State did not have ultimate authority over an individual. When the State claimed such authority, as it did when it compelled people to swear, then the State was attempting to usurp a role reserved for the divine. Laws, especially those laws requiring an oath, do not eliminate the scriptural ban on oaths. In fact, statutes are to be judged in light of the scripture, not vice versa, according to Menno Simons.

> Before these words of Christ all Human laws and policies concerning swearing must stand back and cease. . . . [One] would rather die than weaken or break the precious gospel of our Lord Jesus Christ . . . by temporal policies.[95]

Menno Simons's opposition to capital punishment was also rooted in the idea that the State did not have the authority to grant and remove life. "It would hardly become a true Christian ruler," he wrote, "to shed blood." Menno's reference to Christian rulers did not refer to Anabaptists in power, but to the fact that all the rulers in Europe claimed to preside over a Christian society. Yet Menno found the death penalty to be inconsistent with any understanding of Christian practice. If the condemned embraced Christianity, then executing the prisoner required one Christian to kill another. To execute an "impenitent" posed problems, as well. In that case, execution ended any chance of the person embracing Christianity, sending the condemned "to suffer and bear the

---

[95]Menno, 518-519.

tortures of the unquenchable burning, the consuming fire, eternal pain, woe, and death."[96] The State simply had no authority to take such actions with such finality if the State claimed to represent Christendom.

Much of Campbell's opposition to the death penalty in *The Glad River* emphasized the punishment as a characteristic of the all-powerful state. When Doops and Kingston visit the condemned Arceneau on death row, they find spartan accommodations that seem to serve motives other than security. Especially ironic was the absence of sheets to prevent suicide. Likewise, when Arceneau's sister sends him a sailor's hat, the jailer doubts if he will be able to allow Arceneau to have it. Prisoners condemned to death have high rates of suicide, according to the jailer.[97]

What is important in the story is not so much that Arceneau died, but that he died at the hands of the State's executioner. The story provides a perfect example of Campbell's use of Anabaptist themes. Like the Anabaptists, Campbell wants the Church to be distinct from the dominant culture and a radical distinction between church and state. However, whereas the Anabaptists thought of the state as a divinely-ordained institution, by the 1980s Campbell saw few redeeming qualities in government. Campbell does not view the Church and the State as two spheres, both established by God, though with different functions. He simply rejects the notion that governments are ordained by God.

While portions of Campbell's fiction use the Anabaptist heritage to comment on religion, other portions use more contemporary models. *The Convention* discusses the schism in the Southern Baptist Convention, using the schism as an opportunity to criticize all institutions, as well as an opportunity to present a model of true religion. Campbell modeled the story on the ongoing and ultimately successful fight by fundamentalists to gain control of the infrastructure of the Southern Baptist Convention.[98] During

---

[96]Ibid., 921.
[97]*The Glad River*, 263.
[98]First interview by author.

the conflict, various interest groups emerged. Those sympathetic with the policy changes were called fundamentalists, while those opposed were called moderates. In the story, the interest groups seem more similar than either side would want to admit. Despite any theological differences, both sides have as their preeminent goal the acquisition of power.[99]

In a meeting of the Women's Caucus, the character of Miriam calls the audience back to its heritage. Her frame of reference, however, is not the years before the schism, but the early years before the Baptist denomination carried so much cultural power. She did not see herself as fighting fundamentalism, because the moderate era was far from the original vision of the early Baptists. "Not enough moderates or fundamentalists care about where we Baptists came from," she said. The political activity, in Miriam's view, did not reflect the goals of "dissenting sisters, and brothers, . . . [who] dared to think their own thoughts, dared to ask questions and dared to defy" the authorities.[100]

Campbell's sense of the irrelevance of the denominational fight appears in his description of the parties involved. Dorcas, who becomes the choice of the women to run for President of the Federal Baptist Church, discusses the controversy with her husband, who fails to understand the conflict or to see any major difference in the goals of the opposing groups.[101]

For example, Campbell has Vernon Hedge, a long-time employee of the Convention and a moderate, visit Dorcas and Excell in their hotel room. Hedge has come by to visit Excell, who

---

[99]For summaries and interpretations of the schism in the Southern Baptist Convention, see: Nancy Ammerman, *Baptist Battles: Social Change and Religious Conflict in The Southern Baptist Convention* (New Brunswick: Rutgers University Press, 1990); Ammerman, ed., *Southern Baptists Observed: Multiple Perspectives on a Changing Denomination* (Knoxville: The University of Tennessee Press, 1993); Bill Leonard, *God's Last and Only Hope* (Grand Rapids: Eerdmans Publishing Company, 1990); and Ellen MacGilvra Rosenberg, *The Southern Baptists: A Subculture in Transition* (Knoxville: The University of Tennessee Press, 1989).

[100]*The Convention*, 113-115.

[101]Ibid., 41.

had been attacked by some people in an effort to intimidate Dorcas's candidacy. Hedge, however, apologizes, claiming part of the responsibility. Why does he feel responsible? He explains that all of the officials in the Convention hold responsibility because they "have been part of all this for forty years."[102] Campbell's criticism is that the religious leaders would build an infrastructure in the first place over which subsequent generations could fight.

Like so much of Campbell's work, *The Convention* attacks the human tendency to invest hope in a temporal structure. His heroes (heroines) in the book are those who distance themselves from any structure. For this reason, Campbell not only portrays the fundamentalists in a negative manner. He portrays all those who have complicity in the conflict as essentially the same. In a private meeting of the women leaders, various people express their plans for empowerment, for taking over the system. Miriam rhetorically asks, "If we make an idol out of ours [our movement], ruled by glands and chromosomes, how are we any different?"[103]

Campbell, then, opposes all aspects of professionalism when it comes to religion. He reminds the reader that any institution has an agenda. In portions of his descriptions of the women, Campbell portrays them as well-educated in the best of the theological tradition. Then, he has a pensive Miriam reflect on what she was like before and after her education, asking if "maybe what they took was better than what they gave?" The professional ministry of the divinity schools, according to Campbell, has an agenda of "alleged enlightenment."[104] This agenda is as self-perpetuating as the fundamentalist agenda. Campbell seems to make no distinction between fundamentalist departures from the authentic religion and educated, urbane departures.

The model minister in *The Convention* is Byron Sutton, the McBride's pastor. The "self-educated" Sutton represents what Campbell finds virtuous in a minister. He had not attempted to

---

[102]Ibid., 182.
[103]Ibid., 123.
[104]Ibid., 123, 125.

gain power in the ecclesiastical system. Rather, he remained content working as the bivocational minister in a small, rural church. While attending New Orleans Baptist Theological Seminary, Sutton argued with a professor who claimed that Baptists had existed since the time of Christ, making them the only authentic denomination. When Sutton argued that Menno Simons founded the Baptists, the professor remained unconvinced. Campbell writes the story to show that "Baptists in America had strayed so far from their simple and gentle ways." Sutton continued his education independently, eventually writing his own dissertation on Baptists' kinship to the Anabaptists. After writing the dissertation, Sutton graded it, and granted himself the degree, "Doctor of Religious Knowledge."[105]

The story adds to Campbell's contrast of true religion and false religion. While people must work within structures, they must see the structure as a tool and nothing else. The sophisticated and well-educated, according to Campbell, have the same inclination to serve an institution as the anti-intellectual fundamentalist. His parody of the Southern Baptist Convention does not simply attack fundamentalism. The book criticizes all religious institutions and structures, and offer an alternative vision.

In many ways, Campbell chose diverse settings for each of his novels. Yet, each book has a common link. The books use different historical settings to tell less about the past and more about Campbell's view of the present. Each book discusses community, the Church, relationships, and religious beliefs that Campbell holds as fundamental.

The books are not written as history books. Campbell neglects many key doctrines of the Anabaptists, especially those beliefs that would seem imposing, such as the ban. He is not writing solely about Anabaptists, however. He is writing about the value of the individual and the danger of any institution. With his use of Anabaptists, poor whites, and a denomination in the midst of a power struggle, Campbell has found models to portray vividly his

---

[105]Ibid., 37-39

concept of true religion. Campbell can be elusive in revealing himself. In these three books, he is less elusive, giving his readers a glimpse into who he is and what he believes.

This non-institutional ecclesiology did not originate with Campbell's novels. He expressed many of these ideas in his 1962 book, *Race and the Renewal of the Church*, as well as in several of his articles. These earlier articles criticize the institutional church, although they imply the possibility of their renewal. The later novels offer very little hope for the institutional churches. Instead, they celebrate the existence of the Church in the actions of people of good will.

Campbell's rejection of the institutional church is not a rejection of the authentic Church or the true Christian community. Nor is his rejection of the institutional church a call for people to boycott participation in those structures. What Campbell wants is an ecclesiological Reformation wherein the authentic Church is radically distinguished from institutional religious structures.

Chapter 4

A Story to Tell:
Campbell's Use of Autobiography

Telling one's story is part of the American heritage. American literature is replete with examples of autobiography, ranging from the slave narratives of those without power, such as *The Narrative of the Life of Frederick Douglass*, to the personal reflections of the nation's social and political elite, as in Benjamin Franklin's *Autobiography*.

Members of the clergy wrote many of the early autobiographies in the United States, composing their life stories for public reading as a means of instructing people in their religion. According to Robert Sayre, even when these autobiographies were not explicitly sectarian, they were "religious" in nature. Sayre categorized all these early chronicles of the self as religious insofar as they deal with essentially religious questions. These authors have tended to approach the religious in two ways: The writings of ministers, such as Jonathan Edwards, John Woolman, Peter Cartwright, or Orestes Brownson, are expressly sectarian. The writings and autobiographies of Benjamin Franklin, Ethan Allen, Henry Thoreau, and Henry Adams are secular writings "with a profoundly religious function." These writers "made a religion of America." All autobiographers, whether secular or sectarian, reflect a religious outlook because they have a goal of "defining and locating the self within the universal designs of God, history, or Providence."

How does autobiography function in society? What does an autobiographer hope to accomplish? Albert Stone stated that autobiography asks and answers the question, "Who are you and how did you come to be that way?" Lawrence Buell writes that autobiography describes a person's thinking and experiences over a long period of time. Using the descriptions of Stone and Buell, Betty Bergland concludes that autobiography deals with "meanings associated with 'self,' 'life,' and 'writing,' linked to the term auto/bio/graphy." She adds that these writings are all set in the wider context of the prevailing culture. Autobiography does not merely chronicle a person's life, but also deals with one's experiences and self-formation in the context of the society at large.[1]

This understanding of autobiography comes forth in the writings and narratives of Will Campbell. In *Brother to a Dragonfly* Campbell describes his place as a child in the Campbell family, writing, "This is who I am." All his books and articles have a sense of personal narrative about them. Even his fiction, which he did not deliberately intend to be autobiographical, reveals something about Campbell's world view. Despite his claim that his novels are not intentional autobiographies, Campbell does admit that every experience shaped him, although the influence in some cases was not a conscious one.[2] These personal experiences are in some form reflected in all his works. Campbell's books treat religious themes and tie into larger events that intersected Campbell's own life, and thus match two of what Sayre considered the distinguishing characteristics of autobiography.

---

[1]On the nature of autobiography, see *Encyclopedia of the American Religious Experience*, s.v. "Religious Autobiography," by Robert F. Sayre, 1223-1226; Betty Bergland, "Autobiography and American Culture," *American Quarterly* 45 (September 1993): 446; For further studies of autobiography, see: Paul John Eakin, ed., *American Autobiography: Retrospect and Prospect* (Madison: University of Wisconsin Press, 1991); Louis Kaplan, et al., *A Bibliography of American Autobiographies* (Madison: University of Wisconsin Press, 1962); James Olney, *Metaphors of Self: The Meaning of Autobiography* (Princeton: Princeton University Press, 1972); James Olney, ed., *Autobiography: Essays Theoretical and Critical* (Princeton: Princeton University Press, 1980); Robert F. Sayre, *The Examined Self: Benjamin Franklin, Henry Adams, Henry James* (Madison: University of Wisconsin Press, 1988); and Albert E. Stone, ed., *The American Autobiography: A Collection of Critical Essays* (Englewood: New Jersey, 1981).

[2]*Brother to a Dragonfly*, 38. Asked if *The Glad River* was autobiographical, Campbell said, "No," but quickly added, "except that everything you write, everything you say is autobiographical in a sense." The novelist Walker Percy, a friend of Campbell's, told Campbell that the character in *The Glad River*, "Doops," was autobiographical. When Campbell denied it, Percy said, "You might not have intended it, but you are." Second interview by author.

Campbell enjoyed writing from childhood, and he sees that profession, along with freelance speaking, as his livelihood. From a professional standpoint, Campbell is far more of a writer than a minister. Since 1962, he has written or edited sixteen books. These books can be divided into three categories: ethical, fictional, and autobiographical. The categories are not mutually exclusive because he utilizes all three approaches in all of his books, although one of these approaches dominates each particular work.[3]

His interest as a writer stemmed from his childhood when, as a forty-seven-pound thirteen-year-old, he was chosen last to play ball with his friends. To save himself from embarrassment, Will often stayed away from the neighborhood games, remaining in his room to write "cowboy stories" modeled on the popular westerns of the day. Eventually, the mature Campbell wrote about his own experiences as means of addressing his audience. He has been satisfied with his work as a writer, pleased that all his books are still in print, with the exception of *Race and the Renewal of the Church*, which remained in print for seventeen years.[4]

Campbell has also become satisfied with being seen as an autobiographer. Formerly seeing autobiography as "presumptuous . . . [and] riddled with hubris," him now sees it as perhaps the most important means of learning from others.[5] Campbell's books, essays, and interviews all reflect something of his own story and self-awareness, both set against the backdrop of the social changes that occurred during his life. The genre of autobiography serves for Campbell as an expression of himself as minister and Southerner, as well as a means to address selected social issues.

---

[3]The ethical writings are: *Race and the Renewal of the Church*, ". . . and the criminals with him . . .* ; The Failure and the Hope: Essays of Southern Churchmen, Up to Our Steeples in Politics, God on Earth: The Lord's Prayer for Our Time*, and *Callings*. The fictional writings are: *Chester and Chun Ling* (children's book), *Covenant, Cecelia's Sin, The Convention: A Parable*; and *The Glad River*. The autobiographical writings are: *Brother to a Dragonfly, Forty Acres and a Goat*, and *Providence*.

[4]Second interview by author.

[5]Dibble interview, 146.

Will Campbell's Self-Awareness as a Minister

Ask Will Campbell what his vocation is and he does not equivocate: he is a preacher. He developed this self-awareness in his childhood, pursued it as a college student and seminarian, and, after a period of disillusionment with institutional religion, embraced it during his work with the NCC and retained it into his maturity. This self-awareness emerges in many of Campbell's writings and interviews. Asked about his conflict with the NCC, Campbell said that the problem stemmed from differing ideas of his job. The executives, he believed, wanted him to be a "social engineer," but he believed he was "a preacher."[6] In *Forty Acres and a Goat*, Campbell recounted his struggle in coming to terms with his religious identity. After considering a change of denominations, Campbell reached a conclusion:

> I resolved to be a Baptist preacher of the South until the day I die. Though never again a Southern Baptist preacher. For the first time I knew there was a difference. And what it was.[7]

In an interview in *The Christian Century*, Campbell referred to himself as "a Baptist preacher, but never on Sunday," adding that some people "get the symbolism of that and others don't."[8]

Campbell wanted to become a minister from his earliest years in childhood. He never recalls seriously considering any other career. When an uncle asked the question often directed at youngsters, "What you gonna be when you grow up . . . ?"

---

[6]Second interview by author.

[7]*Forty Acres and a Goat*, 148. In the second interview with the author, Campbell also made almost the same statement when asked if he was comfortable being a Baptist. "I even think of myself as a Baptist preacher. But a Baptist preacher of the South, not a Southern Baptist preacher, and I know the difference." Second interview by author.

[8]"Living Out the Drama: An Interview with Will Campbell," interview by Kenneth L. Gibble, *The Christian Century*, 30 May 1984, 572.

Campbell answered, "B'lieve I'll be a preacher."[9] Family and social influences undoubtedly pushed Campbell in this direction. Campbell's family was active in the East Fork Baptist Church, and his parents, especially his mother, had made a vow when Campbell was ill with pneumonia that if he recovered, he would enter the ministry. As a child, Campbell was the one chosen to pray at meals—"without any choice in the matter"—which served as a familial endorsement of his calling.[10] In Campbell's assessment of his decision to become a minister, he said, "I was always going to be a preacher."[11]

Despite the strong cultural and parental influence, Campbell seemed comfortable with the decision to enter the ministry. After he preached his first sermon, he not only felt that the community accepted him in the ministerial role but also that he had established an individual identity. He became especially aware for the first time of having an identity distinct from that of his brother. Becoming a minister established Campbell as Will Campbell, rather than Joseph Campbell's brother. Campbell recalled, "Now I could claim a success of my own." Despite the problems that Campbell later encountered with institutional religion, he retains the ministerial self-awareness. Indeed, Campbell claimed that he "never doubted or questioned the call." His doubts did not involve his sense of being a minister, but rather his sense that the institutional church did not provide him a place to be faithful to that calling as he understood it. Campbell saw himself as having "a call but no steeple."[12]

The act of being ordained as a minister has played an important role in Campbell's self-awareness. In *Brother to a Dragonfly*, Campbell paints a vivid image of his ordination service, recalling the friends and relatives who laid their hands on his head, "setting

---

[9]*Forty Acres and a Goat*, 2-3.
[10]*Brother to a Dragonfly*, 57.
[11]Campbell, interview by Caudill, 8.
[12]*Brother to a Dragonfly*, 78; *Forty Acres and a Goat*, 6.

me apart to the Gospel ministry."[13] The certificate of ordination was a primitive document with misspelled words, typed by the student pastor who officiated at the service. Campbell for a time was embarrassed by the certificate when he was a student and young pastor. When he eventually developed the awareness that his vocation as a "preacher" surpassed any institutional affiliation that he had, Campbell came to prize the document. As an act embodying his sense of calling, Campbell gathered numerous certificates and diplomas into a single frame and glued his ordination certificate on top.[14]

The importance of Campbell's ordination is also evident in his recollection of a brief attempt by the congregation to withdraw his ordination. When Campbell became increasingly involved in the civil rights movement, some people in his home congregation no longer wanted the church to endorse him as a minister. Campbell recalled two things that prevented the removal of his ordination: the church did not know the proper way to withdraw an ordination, and several people in the community rallied to Campbell's defense vowing, "If you try to unordain Will Davis, we'll come up there and filibuster 'till Hell freezes over." Anxious to avoid further controversy, the congregation dropped all discussion of rescinding Campbell's ordination.

The sense of calling to the ministry in general is not a sufficient image of Campbell's self-awareness. Campbell understood himself not only as a preacher, but as a Baptist preacher. While enrolled at Yale Divinity School from 1949-1952, Campbell considered becoming a Methodist minister. His enrollment in a Methodist polity course provided him a chance to become familiar with that ecclesiastical structure. Campbell's interest in social issues, an interest that drew him to Yale, had caused him to question his ability to survive in a Southern Baptist pulpit. Remaining in the

---

[13]*Brother to a Dragonfly*, 129.

[14]Caudill interview, 6-7. In a 1992 interview with Campbell at his Tennessee home, this author viewed the ordination certificate, displayed prominently in the Campbell home.

North and finding a progressive Baptist congregation was not an option for Campbell. "My commitment," he said, "was really more to the South than it was to the Baptist Church."

On a visit to his home in Amide County during his seminary years, Campbell visited with the Methodist Bishop of Louisiana about the prospect of becoming a Methodist minister. The Bishop promised Campbell a congregation after his graduation and told him that the Methodist Church could accept his ordination. When he returned to Yale, Campbell passed an examination in Methodist polity and made plans to have his ordination transferred to the Methodist Church during an Annual Conference in New York. Campbell traveled to a church in New York where the ordination was to take place. Standing with a group of fifteen to twenty ministerial candidates, Campbell was the last in the processional heading into the sanctuary. At the last minute, he changed his mind, convinced that expediency was not a good reason to switch denominations. Instead of going into the church, he turned, went out a side door, and took a train back to New Haven.[15]

Shortly after Campbell moved to the Nashville area in 1956, he "carried on a brief flirtation with the Episcopal Church." Campbell and his family moved to the community of Donelson, and the local Baptist pastor paid him a visit. The Sunday following the visit, the pastor told his congregation that "someone had moved into the neighborhood to tear up the Baptist Church." At that time, Campbell still had a desire to attend conventional Sunday services, but he did not want to subject his family to the possibility of harassment by the pastor and church members. He also did not want to expose his children to what he felt would be his own negative reactions Sunday after Sunday.

A friend of Campbell's served as the rector of an Episcopal mission in Donelson, and Campbell decided to attend that church. Eventually, Campbell and his family decided to be baptized and

---

[15]For all information on Campbell's ordination, see second interview by author, 28-29. At the time Campbell was not aware of the attempt to remove his ordination. "[M]y father didn't tell me for many years, until it was all over."

confirmed in the Episcopal Church. Because the Episcopal Church had more rigid ordination requirements than the Methodist Church, Campbell was not able to transfer his Baptist orders.

The rector, however, encouraged Campbell to become a lay reader so that he could speak at the mission's services. As Campbell recalled, the Episcopal Church had two levels of lay reader. The basic category allowed the lay reader to preach sermons that had been composed by someone else. A more advanced level allowed the lay reader to compose and preach sermons. It was this advanced level that the Bishop conferred on Campbell.

Meanwhile, some people in the area opposed to Campbell's work with the NCC began following him to the churches where he was to speak. These protesters informed members of the various congregations that Campbell was not ordained as an Episcopal, which was true, and that he was impersonating an Episcopal priest, which was false. Campbell allowed himself to be introduced as an ordained minister because he had not renounced his Baptist ordination. He did not, however, claim to be an Episcopal priest. According to Campbell, the people called him "a fraud and a phony and an impostor, all of which I probably was, but not for the reason they said."

To resist the efforts of his opponents, Campbell had some cards printed, which he distributed at his speaking engagements. The cards read, "Will D. Campbell (I am not now, nor have I ever been, an Episcopal priest.)" When the bishop became involved in the matter, Campbell wrote to him to deny making any claim of being an Episcopal priest. "I sent word to the Bishop," Campbell recalled, "that not only did I not claim to be an Episcopal priest, but knowing some of them as I did, if I were one I would be more inclined to deny it." According to Campbell, "The Bishop didn't think that was very funny," and did not renew Campbell's status as a lay reader.

Despite the setback, Campbell felt that he was able to use humor once again to defend himself. Soon after he lost his license as a lay reader, he was addressing a group of ministerial students at The University of the South in nearby Sewanee, Tennessee. He announced to the audience that he was "the only deposed lay reader in the history of Canterbury." When he finished his speech, a professor informed him that lay readers cannot be deposed since they do not have status as ordained ministers. Rather, they have their licenses revoked. "You are crazy as hell," I told him, "if you think I'm going to let my children grow up thinking their father has been revoked. That's common. Being deposed has some class about it."[16]

That experience ended Campbell's explorations into different Christian denominations. He decided that all denominations, as institutional structures, were alike in limiting personal freedom. From a positive perspective, Campbell decided that he was comfortable with being a renegade Baptist preacher.

It is the symbolism of the Baptist preacher that appeals to Campbell, not the literal practice of the ministry as a profession. Campbell left each position in a professional ministry disillusioned and uninterested in finding another similar ministry. While the symbolism of A Baptist ministry conveyed freedom to Campbell, the ministry as it played itself out in reality conveyed a loss of personal control. In describing his feelings as a parish minister, Campbell said he was treated as a "mascot." He joked that his wife often said "the only reason she'd ever leave me would be if I took another parish church," to which Campbell replied, "I don't think there's any danger of that. . . . I've never been considered for another one."[17]

Campbell consciously worked to see that his work differed from more conventional ministries. Although he had the potential to develop a formal organization with followers, Campbell has

---

[16]For all information on Campbell's "flirtation" with the Episcopal Church, see *Forty Acres and a Goat*, 146-147; Second interview by author. Humor and candid observations are part of Campbell's method of social observation, as well as part of himself. By the time he began writing novels and autobiographies, Campbell was able to use this convention to discuss very painful memories of his personal life, as well as his disillusionment with his role as a conventional social activist. The use of humor is strongest, however, in *Forty Acres and a Goat*.

[17]Second interview with author.

discouraged any moves in that direction. Not wanting to promote himself as a guru, Campbell wrote, "I'm trying to be a disciple, not attract them."[18]

In addition to avoiding the development of a personality cult, Campbell has criticized institutional ministries that he believed moved in that direction. One ministry that received criticism from Campbell was that of Billy Graham. In 1973, Campbell wrote an article for *Katallegete* entitled, "Can there is a Crusade for Christ?" Borrowing the word "crusade" from the title of Graham's mass evangelism rallies, the article concluded that traditional evangelism and Christianity stood in conflict. Graham's institutional approach to religion, as well as that of other mass evangelists, was not a valid interpretation of the New Testament. Thirteen years later, in *Forty Acres and a Goat*, he reminisced about his opinion of Graham, noting ways that his assessment of Graham and his organization had changed.

In the book, Campbell recalled a Graham crusade in Nashville that coincided with the recent publication of Marshall Frady's unflattering biography of the evangelist. Frady devoted an entire chapter to Campbell in his journalistic book, comparing the differing approaches of these two very different Baptist ministers to the Christian ministry. Because of Frady's book, people from Graham's advance team in Nashville contacted Campbell, asking him if he planned to attend the services. When Campbell declined to attend, the advance team continued to call, telling Campbell that Graham desired a private meeting.

On the last day of the crusade, Campbell finally agreed to meet with Graham. He had once considered Graham "the worst of the religious and political right" due to the evangelist's early attacks that, in Campbell's view, "equated Communism with the devil, [and] America with the Kingdom of God on earth." By 1979, Campbell's views of Graham had mellowed. While he continued to reject the evangelist's institutional approach to religion, Campbell sensed a maturity in Graham's views evidenced by his

---

[18]*Forty Acres and a Goat*, 189.

more recent denunciations of nuclear war. Campbell described Graham as "a modest and charming gentleman," as well as "a man of honor and integrity." While Campbell rejected the Graham institutional ministry, he felt he could accept Graham as a person.[19]

Campbell also defies traditional understandings of the ministry in his use of crude language. Many of Campbell's interviews, books, and articles are laced with deliberately chosen expletives. Campbell uses forceful language to show how his ministerial identity has little to do with traditional notions of personal piety. In *Forty Acres and a Goat*, the character T. J. Jackson asked Campbell, "Why do you use such dirty language?"

To answer the question, Campbell told a story about a friend's appearance on a radio program. A caller to the program asked Thad Garner, the pseudonym for Campbell's friend and fellow minister, his opinion of the use of vulgar language by Johnny Cash on a television program. When Garner asked the caller what the word was, the caller refused to say it. Garner then announced that he would name three words and the caller could identify which one Cash used on television. When Garner listed the words, "death," "nuclear war," and "electric chair," the caller hung up.

> I'm sorry you left us, ma'am. . . . That's three of the nastiest, filthiest, ugliest, most vile words I know. If Johnny Cash didn't say any of those, and if you can't tell me what he did say, well, I guess I can't help you.[20]

To this story, Campbell added that he used shocking language "to make a point" that all language is "relative." Campbell felt that the actions of a minister, and a practicing Christian, involved one's

---

[19]On Campbell's views of Billy Graham, see Campbell and James Y. Holloway, "Can There Be a Crusade for Christ?" *Katallegete*, Summer 1973, 2-6; Marshall Frady, *Billy Graham, a Parable of American Righteousness* (Boston: Little, Brown, 1979); *Forty Acres and a Goat*, 159-161, 164.

[20]*Forty Acres and a Goat*, 186.

treatment of other humans.[21] He would not deny that some language might not be appropriate for certain audiences, but Campbell would base such a decision on social conventions, not Christianity.

As Campbell has defined the Christian ministry, then, he is comfortable with the identity of being a minister or preacher. He sees institutional ministry and authentic ministry as two different entities. To those who do not consider his approach to be valid ministry, Campbell said, "They must not read the New Testament very closely." The public acceptance of his ministry, as well as the approval of a traditional denomination, has no bearing on Campbell's ministerial self-awareness. He admittedly does not fit the cultural stereotype of a minister and has no desire to. For him, however, a minister is one "who participates in a service, a litany, someone who supports others and holds them up and celebrates life and expresses hope and resurrection," all of which Campbell believes that he does. Campbell argues,

> I do ten times more of what is traditionally called the parish ministry or the pastoral ministry; that's burying people, marrying people, counseling . . . sick people . . . than I ever did while I was under the canopy of the steeples, or while I was in the structure of the institutional church.

Campbell considers himself a minister and does not think that his departure from the institutional church has violated the terms of his ordination. He views himself as more in accord with his ordination than ever and holds that his ordination council would approve of the direction his non-institutional ministry:

> I think overall they would say, "Yeah, I think the old boy is pretty much being faithful to what we had in mind for

---

[21]Ibid., 159.

him to do when we turned him loose out there in the world."[22]

Autobiography and Campbell's Social Concerns

In his writings and interviews Campbell addresses a number of ethical issues from a personal, narrative point of view. Rather than merely editorializing, he discusses particular issues both in the larger social context and against the background of his personal experiences. Several issues illustrate this approach.

Race relations from an explicitly Christian perspective contin-ued to occupy a place in Campbell's self-reflection. He considered racial animosity as a continuing problem in America (not just the South) and the source of many of the nation's other problems. In 1979 Campbell told a group of Tennessee educators that race remained "the most crucial issue" in American education. Camp-bell also considered race relations to be a continuing problem in the churches. Noting the efforts by civil rights activists to desegre-gate churches in the 1960s, Campbell lamented that by the 1980s the churches remained segregated. He also commented that segregation appears to be the choice of whites and African Ameri-cans."[23]

While he stopped short of labeling racial problems as inherent in society, he did not dismiss the possibility. As an example, Campbell listed the irony of the state of Mississippi, a poor state, casting the largest plurality for the Republican presidential candidate in 1992. According to Campbell, the logical vote for a poor region would be a vote for a liberal to progressive party. That Mississippi did not vote accordingly could only stem from continued racial division.

[Mississippi] gave George Bush the greatest plurality of any state in the Union. The poorest state in the country. Makes

---

[22]On his "pastoral ministry," see Caudill interview, 86,98-100.

[23]"Our Adolescent History," 40; *Forty Acres and a Goat*, 28.

no sense in the world for that state going Republican. And it's spelled R-A-C-E and that's the only reason for it.[24]

During the 1980s, Campbell wrote a number of articles for *Christianity and Crisis* that addressed ethical issues using an autobiographical motif. These articles dealt with the range of issues that concerned the mature Campbell, including race relations, the death penalty, nuclear weapons, and women in ministry, to name a few.

In a March 17, 1986 article, Campbell reminisced about the recent commemoration for the first time of Martin Luther King's birthday as a national holiday. Campbell started the article by recalling that his grandmother said "that funerals and weddings bring on a lot of changes." His grandmother also told him that "no house had ever been built big enough for two families." The two sayings of his grandmother provided Campbell with a view to evaluate American society since the life and death of King. That the country celebrated the holiday caused Campbell to see some signs of improvement and "change" in American society.

Campbell also used the King holiday to reflect on his limited role at the founding of King's organization, The Southern Christian Leadership Conference. The SCLC was formed in January 1957 at a meeting in Atlanta, Georgia. The meeting grew out of a successful boycott of public transportation in Montgomery, Alabama, coordinated by King and the Montgomery Improvement Association. The movement's success in that city motivated African Americans across the South to meet in Atlanta and form a regional organization.

Because he was employed by the NCC as a specialist in race relations, Campbell attended the organizational meeting of the new group, the only white person present. He was present as an observer, not a delegate. In addition to organizing, the delegates adopted a working statement entitled, "A Statement to the South and Nation." Campbell used his 1986 article to consider the

---

[24]Second interview by author.

proposals of that 1957 document written several years before the civil rights struggle began in earnest. The statement called the United States "a beacon of hope for the oppressed peoples of the world." It also encouraged President Eisenhower to deliver a speech in the South calling for the end of segregation and for Vice President Nixon to tour the South on the same behalf, as he had done for "Hungarian refugees." The plea that the document directed to the country's leaders went unheeded, but Campbell proposed that if the national leadership had accepted the proposals in 1957, "we might be reading a different world history."[25]

In 1985 Campbell wrote another article, filled with personal experiences, opposing abortion and the death penalty. Ideological approaches to these issues generally had a person opposing one and supporting the other. Religious and political conservatives often supported the use of the death penalty and opposed abortion rights. People on the opposite end of the spectrum who supported abortion rights often opposed the death penalty.

To illustrate his point, Campbell recalled appearing on a radio program when a caller praised James Earl Ray, the assassin of Martin Luther King, Jr. The program hostess was so upset that she became ill and played a commercial. The next day, however, the hostess endorsed the death penalty on the air. In the same article, Campbell recalled approaching a protester marching in support of right wing causes. Asking the person his feelings on abortion and the death penalty, Campbell discovered that the young man believed abortion to be a sin and the death penalty to be sanctioned by scripture.

Campbell aimed in his article to show how a political approach to these issues involving life and death divided natural allies. Of the experiences he described, Campbell asked, "What do all those things mean?" He then offered an answer.

----

[25]"Movement Hangover," *Christianity and Crisis*, 17 March 1986, 77-88; *Dictionary of Christianity in America*, s.v. "Southern Christian Leadership Conference," by T. R. Peake; Campbell, second interview by author.

[M]aybe if those of us who are concerned with one or another of those issues, but suspect or detest those concerned with the others, learned . . . to cry in the same towel, we might become friends too. With more in common than we often think.[26]

Among the social issues that have concerned Campbell since his departure from work in the institutional church has been the treatment of prisoners. Campbell's approach to prisoners and crime in society is the most radical of all his activities. Campbell takes literally the passage in Luke 4 that records Jesus as saying that he has come "to proclaim release for prisoners." In Campbell's estimation, the release proclaimed extends to all prisoners regardless of their crimes.

Both Testaments understand all prisoners to be *political* prisoners. Murderers, rapists, sodomists, insurrectionists, assassins, thieves of millions in a stock fraud or of a loaf of bread to keep the family alive.[27]

Out of this perspective, Campbell related his autobiographical account of a trip to San Francisco with his wife on the occasion of their forty-first wedding anniversary. Among the places he toured was the former federal prison, Alcatraz, located on an island in San Francisco Bay. As Campbell toured the empty cells, he thought of the empty prison as "a happy reminder that Easter is coming." He also felt that "if Christ had spoken the truth he had been in those cells too."

While on the tour, Campbell found a book in the prison's souvenir store that quoted Robert Kennedy's words on the occasion of the prison's closing. Kennedy called for the future penal system in the country "to balance the needs of deterrent and

---

[26]"On Getting Sick Together," *Christianity and Crisis*, 1 April 1985, 100-102.

[27]Campbell and James Y. Holloway, *". . . and the criminals with him. . ."* (New York: Paulist Press, 1973), 141.

detention with the possibilities of rehabilitation." Campbell compared these words with the conditions at the Marion, Illinois prison that replaced Alcatraz. Reminding the readers that the Marion facility had been under a "complete lockdown" for four years, Campbell described the prison's conditions, which included isolation in the cells and the wearing of handcuffs whenever prisoners left their quarters. To these conditions, Campbell asked, "What happened to the noble intentions of the Attorney General?"[28]

Campbell also used his autobiographical reflections in *Christianity and Crisis* to discuss the role of women in ministry. The personal context of this interest was the enrollment in divinity school of one of Campbell's daughters. The larger context that drew Campbell into this social issue involved the opposition to female ministers in many churches, particularly in the Southern Baptist Convention.

Campbell began a 1985 article on the subject of women in ministry with a reference to an Anabaptist woman, Maeyken Wens, who was put to death in 1573 for preaching contrary to the teachings of the state church. After describing the details of Maeyken Wens's martyrdom, Campbell mentioned that "Maeyken's spiritual relatives" had met during the annual Southern Baptist Convention of 1984 and passed a resolution condemning the ordination of women as ministers.

Campbell attacked the SBC resolution with two statements, one sarcastic and the other serious. First, Campbell questioned the logic of the resolution, which claimed that one reason for the exclusion of women from ministry was that a literal reading of the creation story in Genesis placed women "first in the Edenic fall." Using humor, Campbell suggested that the feminine role in the fall of humanity could have a different outcome.

One might think that since they have been at it [sin] longer they would be more competent in identifying and casting

---

[28]"Tourist Notes," *Christianity and Crisis*, 16 March 1987, 85-86.

it out. But logic has never carried much weight where mischief and foolishness reign.

On a more serious note, Campbell noted that the denial of ordination to women among Baptists denied the Anabaptist heritage of modern Baptists. This denial also ignored the fact that women were already serving as ministers regardless of the endorsement of a parent denomination. "[T]hat resolution," affirmed Campbell, "will no more stop their mothers and sisters from declaring the mighty acts of God . . . than the tongue screws stopped" the female Anabaptist ministers of an earlier era.[29]

One year later, Campbell addressed the ordination of women in yet another essay he wrote for *Christianity and Crisis*. He used the same personal, narrative form of autobiography to address this larger issue. Campbell opened this article quoting some lines from a country music song entitled, "Digging Up Bones." The part of the song that leads into his article is, "exhuming things that's better left alone."

For Campbell, that which should have been left alone was a new policy by the Home Mission Board of the Southern Baptist Convention that banned denomination funds from mission churches that ordained women. Campbell opposed the policy not only because he thought it was sexist but also because he believed that the Pauline passages used in support of the policy were misinterpretations of Paul's thought.

On an autobiographical note, Campbell noted how he had often explained the Pauline statement in 1Corinthians 14: 34-35, a passage that some understand as forbidding women to speak in church services, allowing them to discuss questions about the service only at home with their husbands. Campbell said that at one time, when the passage came up, he "kept an embarrassed silence," or he explained the passage as no longer relevant because it was rooted in distinct cultural mores which have been superseded in the modern world

---

[29]"On Silencing Our Finest," 340-341.

Now, Campbell no longer understands the passage as a Pauline ban against women ministers rooted in a cultural context. Rather, Campbell concluded that the words were not Paul's view on women, but Paul's restatement of the views of some of the Corinthians who had written him earlier. Paul quoted the passage condemning women in a move to condemn that view. The work of Charles Talbert, a professor at Baylor University, reinforced Campbell in his new understanding of Paul. Campbell read an article in *SBC Today* by Talbert that "reminded" Campbell of a different interpretation of Paul.

After describing how his thinking about the Pauline view of women had changed, Campbell wondered why the false understanding of Paul had been continued by religious leadership he felt should know better. He also thought the issue demonstrated the danger of using God to validate a personal, social viewpoint. Campbell believed that many religious views, including opposition to women in ministry, were actually cultural views already held by some people. These people then looked to conservative, popular religion to endorse their already held cultural views.

> Maybe that matter [the ordination of women], as well as a lot of other biblical illiteracy being peddled in the name of biblical inerrancy and biblical literalism, is a conspiracy of the devils. Get the good church folk to believe you are speaking for God and you have won the battle.

Campbell closed his article with some strong, personal reflections on the position of the Home Mission Board of his denomination. First, he wondered why anyone "would even *want* to be ordained in an institution which has so subverted the Gospel." Second, Campbell questioned whether ordination as practiced by most denominations reflects the concept of ministry put forth in the teachings of Jesus. Finally, Campbell challenged the theology of the Home Mission Board in its actions against women ministers.

I am even more hard pressed to see his [Jesus'] spirit in the action of the rulers of the Home Mission Board of my Holy Mother Church. . . . And many others of similar ilk. . . . Better [to] have left that verse alone, for it will some day come back to haunt them. Maybe even in hell for abusing the Word, and children, of God.[30]

Campbell has also used personal narrative to address his concerns about nuclear armaments. An article in *Christianity and Crisis* that he wrote was set against a 1985 arms summit between Ronald Reagan and Mikhail Gorbachev. Campbell used most of the space in the four-column article discussing stories about his young grandson. The last two paragraphs used the warmth Campbell attempted to evoke in the readers to suggest a possible solution to international tension. Suggesting that the tensions between the United States and the Soviet Union could be solved through a "grandchild exchange," Campbell recommended that the President's grandchildren spend time in the Soviet Union and the Secretary General's grandchildren spend time in the United States. Although his proposal was, of his own admission, a "nonsense solution," Campbell used the idea to make his point about nuclear warfare. Campbell did not think his proposal for a grandchild exchange would be accepted by the world's political leaders. However, exchanging grandchildren as a means of solving political differences, Campbell argued, is "not as nonsensical as blowing up the universe to settle something that would no longer need settling."[31]

Three years before his article in *Christianity and Crisis*, Campbell addressed nuclear warfare in an essay for *The Progressive*. Campbell used a personal tragedy and a national tragedy as a starting point to argue his belief that nuclear warfare was senseless. The personal tragedy for Campbell was the poisoning of his dog by some unknown assailant, an act he considered senseless. The

---

[30]"Quit Picking on Paul," *Christianity and Crisis*, 8 December 1986, 428-430.
[31]"Summit Wishes," *Christianity and Crisis*, 23 December 1985, 508-510.

national tragedy that Campbell mentioned was the 1985 Tylenol murders. Like the person or persons who poisoned his dog, the person or persons who laced Tylenol capsules with cyanide "placed no value on human life." After describing the personal and national tragedy, Campbell stated that "the event demands that we reflect upon some other aspects of our troubled world."

Campbell then used Tylenol as an analogy of the danger posed by nuclear weapons. He drew a number of comparisons between the Tylenol murderer, the pharmaceutical industry, and nuclear weaponry. As a result of the deaths, the company manufacturing Tylenol suffered a great profit loss. While Campbell expressed no sorrow at the damage done to the corporate structure, he did express "care for the thousands whose living depends upon that corporate structure."

He also noted that, sadly, much of the national economy had become dependent on the defense industry for its livelihood. Also, he noted that national defense policy rested on a willingness to use nuclear weapons with the belief that the Soviet Union would not go to war against the United States out of a fear of a mutual destruction. These observations formed the basis of Campbell's Tylenol analogy. Just as the Tylenol murderer had no regard for human life and did not know the victims, likewise the national leaders advocating the use of nuclear weapons do not know the potential victims and are not acting out of a regard for human life. Campbell asked, "So who's tampering with the Tylenol now? And who has no regard at all for human life?"

Campbell next drew a larger lesson from the Tylenol murders. He noted that Tylenol does not cure illnesses, it only relieves and sometimes masks symptoms. For Campbell, the patriotism associated with building public support for nuclear weapons does not cure national problems, it only masks symptoms.

> The strategic Tylenols, the world's nuclear stockpiles, do ease certain pains of the sick human race. They lull us, nation to armed nation, into a sense of security and

superiority and deceive us. . . . But these over-the-counter drugs simply tend to mask our symptoms and cure nothing.

Into this "capsule of patriotism and nationalism" has been inserted the "cyanide" of nuclear warfare, he argued. Just as the makers of Tylenol assumed that their product would always be in safe hands, even so the scientists who produce nuclear weapons assume that these instruments will always be in the hands of the rational leaders. Of nuclear weapons, Campbell wrote, "We have not reckoned with the possibility of tampering." Campbell closed his personal narrative against nuclear warfare by warning that "[t]he greatest danger the nations face is that someone will tamper with the Tylenol of defense. A product that cures nothing. And kills everyone."[32]

Campbell's Self-Awareness as a Southerner

Will Campbell has been shaped by Southern culture. He identified with the American South and chose to remain in the South despite that region's social mores. Campbell's iconoclastic introduction to an audience viewing a documentary—"I'm a Baptist preacher. I'm a native of Mississippi. And I'm pro-Klansman because I'm pro-human being"—captures the tensions in Campbell's self-awareness as a Southerner. Campbell has not blindly celebrated all of southern culture, just as he has not embraced all that the Baptist identity entails. However, a sense of southernness permeates Campbell's world view. In the same manner that he embraced Baptist and Anabaptist concepts, Campbell has embraced his southern culture both as a method of expressing himself and as an effort to embrace, rather than deny, his own cultural heritage.

Campbell's interest in the South is not entirely new. Geographically, Campbell has been a part of the South the vast majority of his adult life. With the exception of his three years at Yale,

---

[32]"The Tylenol of Defense," *The Progressive*, 66.

Campbell lived and worked in the South, and since 1956 when he left his job with the NCC, Campbell's work has been directly related to addressing social issues in the South. His years at Yale, moreover, do not represent an attempt to move out of his southern culture. Rather, Campbell was drawn to Yale because of the reputation of some of its faculty. Campbell thought a theological education from Yale would enhance his ability to work in the South as a socially active minister. His intentions were always to return to the South as a pastor after graduation. Indeed, so eager was Campbell to return to the South to engage in faith-based social action that he worried that the Supreme Court would hand down its desegregation ruling in *Brown vs. Board of Education* and he would have no great issues to address from the pulpit. In *Brother to a Dragonfly*, Campbell remarked that he felt "a certain allegiance to our Southland" despite his opposition to the racial mores of the region.[33]

The personal tie to the South also shaped Campbell's choice of jobs when he left the pastorate at Taylor, Louisiana. Offered a position at the University of Oklahoma and a similar one at the University of Mississippi, Campbell chose Mississippi. In looking back on his decision, Campbell remarked, "I think that the reason why I chose Ole Miss was that this was home." Campbell stated that he "always had very strong emotional ties" to the South, especially to his native Mississippi. At this point in his life, his interest in returning did not seem related to Oxford's connection with southern writers, especially William Faulkner. Campbell simply wanted to come home.

Campbell wanted to retain his southern identity even though he returned to the region as a social activist. He felt that much of the social activism of his day was governed as much by cultural values as by humanitarian concerns. Thus, Campbell believed that social activists from the South, including himself, were often forced

---

[33]Second interview by author; In 1979, he mentioned this concern to a group of educators in Tennessee and said, "Here we are, still preaching about it." See "Our Adolescent History," 40; *Brother to a Dragonfly*, 201.

to deny their own heritage. For Campbell, the experience at Yale inhibited his ability to relate to the people of his region. "The very education that I thought was going to prepare me to best minister to . . . 'my people' is the thing that cut me off from it."[34]

Campbell addressed his sense of southernness and the tensions of being a social progressive in the South during a 1979 symposium. Entitled "Sense of Place: Mississippi," the meeting had more than 250 participants and a number of speakers from numerous backgrounds. The goal of the meeting, which culminated in the publication of the keynote addresses, was "understanding what a sense of place is and how it is experienced in Mississippi."[35]

Campbell called his presentation, "Staying Home or Leaving," and the title reflects the dilemma Campbell faced in his southern identity. By 1979 when Campbell delivered his address, he was fully comfortable with being a Southerner. Campbell believed that a sense of place involved "tragedy" as well as triumph. For this reason, his native state and those with ties to it had a strong sense of place. "[B]efore one can understand what the term 'sense of place' means," Campbell said, that person "must first understand the nature of tragedy. Mississippi does have a deep sense of place because Mississippi has a sense of tragedy and suffering."[36]

As a minister and social activist, Campbell wanted to address the social issues that he believed were tragic. He wanted his concern for the suffering of the South to grow out of his southern identity, not to clash with his southern identity. A drawn back to the South during his Yale years, Campbell did not return merely to be near the familiar. Campbell believed that "the tragedy of the South would occupy the remainder of . . . [his] days."[37] He concluded that his personal efforts to address the social issues of his region drew him closer to that region. For Campbell, a healthy

---

[34]Caudill interview, 33.
[35]Peggy W. Prenshaw and Jessie O. McKee, eds., *Sense of Place: Mississippi* (Jackson: University Press of Mississippi, 1979), 2.
[36]"Staying Home or Leaving," 15-16.
[37]*Brother to a Dragonfly*, 98.

and strong tie to a region, like happiness, requires an experience with "heartbreak." "No one—not one—in this room," he told those present at the conference, "feels more keenly than I do a deep and abiding sense of place when the name Mississippi is heard. . . ."[38] Campbell went on to describe what formed that attraction to his home. The South, and Mississippi in particular, attracted him not only because of pleasant memories but also because of bad ones. The tragedy of the region, with its poverty, racial divisions, and violence, created a somber attachment to the area.

> [T]hat love, that sense of place . . . has been forged on the altar of our common suffering much more than on some romantic notion of ease, contentment and tranquillity.[39]

Campbell's sense of place and southernness, then, was connected with his understanding of the South's tragedy. The tragedy he saw extended beyond the obvious issue of race relations. In his mature thought, Campbell addressed the tragedy of the South by discussing a variety of issues, especially the plight of poor southern whites. He also engaged in autobiographical reflection on the tragedy of the region, discussing the tensions of being a socially progressive Southerner, and the ways that orientation cut him off from his own cultural identity.

Campbell's new concern for the plight of the poor white Southerner, including those who belonged to the Ku Klux Klan, grew out of his new awareness that these people reflected the symptoms of racism, not the causes. He also came to believe that improving race relations required more than the presence of whites of goodwill in the African American community. Progressive whites needed to reach out to those people in the white community who had racist ideologies. "If you are interested in trying to improve relationships with the races," Campbell said, "then you go where

---

[38]"Staying Home or Leaving," 15-16.
[39]Ibid.

the problem is."[40] The problem, according to Campbell, was not in the African American community. The problems of racism in American society originated in the white community, and white supporters of improved race relations needed to exert more efforts there. "[T]he problem was in the white community. . . ." Campbell said. "I've seen a lot of white preachers go to the black church and preach on race relations and get back to their church . . . and [then they are] not going to talk about it there."[41]

Campbell was also interested in reaching out to the poor whites in order to avoid making them a scapegoat for the racial ills of the South and nation. Since this group rarely, if ever, wielded power enough to shape society, Campbell concluded that they were victims. Their lack of power and their victimization made them natural allies with the dispossessed African Americans, but their racism prevented the development of this alliance, which added to the tragedy of the South's poor whites.

In a 1980 speech, Campbell developed this theme in detail, using the sayings of Jesus in Matthew 27 as a starting point. This passage records Jesus describing the Pharisees as painted tombs, pleasant on the outside, but putrefied on the inside. It also mentions the irony of their adherence to Jewish dietary laws with regard to the ritual washing of cups over against their neglect of fellow human beings. The poor whites of the Klan, Campbell argued, received far too much attention as victimizers and too little as victims. The Klan is on "the outside of the cup." While the teachings of Jesus do not neglect the "outside," they also "talk about what is inside the sepulcher." Campbell asked, "What is inside the sepulcher which we sometimes forget in our zeal to stop the menace of the KKK?"[42] After listing several social problems and violent actions that had recently occurred, Campbell took aim at what he considered to be inside the sepulcher, namely, the forces of social and political power in the South.

---

[40]Second interview by author.
[41]Ibid.
[42]"Clean Up the Botulism," *Southern Exposure*, Summer 1980, 99.

Let's talk about the resurgence of the Ku Klux Klan in the weeks and months to come in this town [Nashville], but let's do it in the context of the resurgence of Exxon and J. P. Stevens, and the resurgence of Nashville's Belle Meade Country Club.[43]

Campbell's compassion for the poor whites of the South was first nurtured in his reading of Howard Fast's *Freedom Road*. As part of his new approach to social issues, Campbell felt he could identify with these people because he came from their ranks. In *Brother to a Dragonfly*, he was able to return to that identity first nurtured in Fast's novel. "The poor whites," Campbell wrote, "the Abner Laits, the Will Boones he [Fast] described, they were my people." Later in that same book, Campbell described the motivations that pushed him to reach out to poor white members of the Klan. This group, which Campbell said that his "colleagues referred to as 'the Enemy,'" he now accepted as part of the tragedy of his heritage. He saw the poor whites, even the Klan members, as "people who were our people."

Whatever they stood for. Whatever they did. In a strange sequence of crosscurrents we were of them and they were of us. Blood of our blood. Our people. And God's people.[44]

Thus, Campbell embraced poor whites and some of the Klansmen as human beings without accepting their ideology. He accepted his own history as a white Southerner whose personal heritage did not place him within the power structure. Finally, Campbell saw these people as part of the tragedy of racism and economic distress. Their violent actions, although deplorable, stemmed from forces they did not control.

Campbell made this point in a 1977 article, "Where to Sit in Scottsboro." The title alluded to Campbell's reflections on a 1977

---

[43]Ibid.
[44]*Brother to a Dragonfly*, 96-97, 249-250.

lawsuit brought by Ruby Bates against the National Broadcasting Corporation for what she considered to be a slanderous portrayal of her in the television movie, *Judge Horton and the Scottsboro Boys*. The movie dramatized the 1931 trial of nine African Americans for the alleged rape of two white women, Ruby Bates and Victoria Price The nine young boys had illegally boarded a freight train crossing Tennessee and Alabama when they were removed from the train. As they were removed from the train, however, two white women were discovered in a corner of the boxcar. Although the women were allegedly prostitutes, they accused the boys of rape. Originally sentenced to death, the young boys eventually gained their freedom, but not without serving substantial time in prison.

Ruby Bates's testimony, which Campbell correctly declared would have been disregarded if made against another white, was accepted as evidence against the boys. That 1931 testimony became the basis of her 1977 lawsuit. Since the court in 1931 charged the young boys with rape and accepted Bates's testimony that she was not a prostitute, she claimed that the film slandered her in its portrayal. After the court dismissed her suit, Campbell used the event to discuss his feelings, using his autobiographical method.

Campbell saw Bates as a victim used by the white power establishment to control the African American community. While she was wrong to have made her charges, Campbell thought the greater evil was in the 1931 court system that accepted her obviously fabricated testimony. He also saw an evil in the economic system that forced a poor white woman into prostitution to supplement her wages in the mill. While the society should not have convicted the young boys and certainly should not have accepted Bates's testimony, it also should not have allowed the conditions that created a Ruby Bates. Campbell's dilemma about where to sit during the 1977 trial referred to his sense that both the convicted young boys and the prostitutes were victims. The true guilty party was the court system. In 1977, he did not know which victim to embrace. In identifying with the poor whites who were often on the front line of racial violence, Campbell hoped to address the structural sources of racism. In the 1960s and 1970s, Campbell felt that the political leadership of the nation did not have the moral authority to turn its energy against the Ku Klux Klan while at the same time pursuing a war in Vietnam. In Campbell's view, "We are a nation of Klansmen."[45] He felt that the South, and especially the poor whites in the Ku Klux Klan, had become scapegoats that allowed the powerful to evade more comprehensive responses to social ills.

As a social progressive, Campbell at one time devoted little of his energy to these poor whites. He called this time his period of "liberal sophistication." His lack of concern for the poor whites did not help the race issue. Rather, Campbell felt that it resulted in his "denying not only the faith . . . [he] professed to hold, but my history and my people." Campbell wrote that he denied this history "like many another white liberal."[46] This denial of his personal history inhibited his ability to change the attitudes of his fellow whites. He hoped that his acceptance of a sense of place in the South would remove that obstacle. Campbell did not affirm only the pleasant, nostalgic aspect of southernness. By grasping a sense of place in the South, Campbell accepted the tragic role of violence in the region, as well as the potential for good. Campbell felt both an increased comfort with his own identity and an increased effectiveness as a Christian social activist.

Campbell's historical novel, *Providence*, also describes his sense of place in the South, with special emphasis on the tragedy of the region and the tragedy of doctrinaire social liberalism. Although the workers at Providence were forced to stop their work and close their medical clinic, their nonprofit organization retained the title to the land. Eventually, Campbell became a member of the board, which met periodically only to satisfy the legal requirements of the charter. When the group decided to give up the land in the 1980s, Campbell suggested that they give the land to the Choctaw Indians

---

[45]*Brother to a Dragonfly*, 248.
[46]Ibid., 222, 225.

since the land was originally theirs and was forcibly taken from them. Although the board liked the idea at first, they eventually decided to sell it to the Department of the Interior. For Campbell, therein was another tragedy—a group of social progressives from an earlier era failing to broaden their scope of concern in another era.[47]

A final means of Campbell's self-expression as a Southerner comes in his affinity for country western music. Campbell recalled that in his early years of ministry, he became "sophisticated, [and] . . . thought you were [only] supposed to listen to Bach fugues and all that."[48] While he retains an appreciation for classical music, Campbell also returned to an appreciation for the country music he "grew up on." Living in Nashville further enabled Campbell to admire country music, as well as to develop friendships with numerous successful and aspiring performers.

Through country music, Campbell had a paradigm to express both his renewed sense of southernness and his criticism of conventional social liberalism. In his speech to the symposium entitled "Sense of Place: Mississippi," Campbell said, "If you are going to talk in terms of a sense of place in the South, what better way than to talk about its music."[49]

Country music also provided Campbell a means of criticizing the social elitism and the theological deficiency of many white social activists. In one of Campbell's first articles written with a satirical tone, Campbell lauded the virtues of country music and criticized the use of folk songs that were popular in the 1960s. Entitled "Snickness Unto Death . . . Folk vs. Contemporary Country Music," the pseudonymous article especially targeted the Student Non-Violent Coordinating Committee. He wrote this article shortly after his perception that even a liberal movement had certain rules and boundaries that one must follow.

-----

[47]Second interview by author; *Providence* (Atlanta: Longstreet Press, 1993), passim.
[48]Ibid.
[49]"Staying Home or Leaving," 20.

Sarcastically, Campbell wrote that social liberals embraced folk music because it is so compatible with the frame of reference of their movement. In folk music, Campbell claimed, "there is always one line and one message everyone must proclaim or he [or she] is not admitted." Describing folk music, Campbell wrote that this type of song "is what they sing . . . at off-campus coffee houses with names sounding like 'The Bitter End.'" Country music, he argued, is the true liberal music because

> . . . there is no *line* everybody in the field must follow, no *message* all must proclaim. Each song and each singer has his [or her] own line and own message and each line and each message is tolerated by his [or her] fellows.

Campbell said that country music is "honest, liberal, and the only true American art form." He added that "it is also theologically sound (sound meaning orthodox)." By theological orthodoxy, Campbell meant that these musicians "know the world is all fouled up, but if you listen to the ever present closing number, the 'song of inspiration,' you will be reminded that any real hope for changing that situation lies beyond the hands of the Steering Committee. Accepting the doctrine of original sin–all people are no good most of the time–they can get along without a line."[50] Country music, then, provided Campbell a means of expression that combined his southernness and his theological outlook. It also served a tool by which Campbell could use humor to criticize his perception of social elitism.

---

[50]David Brett, "Snickness Unto Death . . . Folk vs. Contemporary Country Music," *Motive*, March 1965, 35-38. Campbell used this pseudonym for no particular reason. One other article by Campbell used the name of a farmer as the author to draw attention to plight of the small farm. Herschel Ligon, "The Pragmatics of Parity," *Christianity and Crisis*, 6 February 1978, 6-8. See also Campbell, fourth interview by author, Phone call, Waco, Texas to Nashville, Tennessee, 21 February 1994.

To sum up, then, one of the dominant characteristics of Will Campbell's writings is their autobiographical element. Campbell has described who he thinks that he is and why he developed in the direction he did. He has set his personal development and self-awareness in the context of developments in the larger culture. Campbell's autobiographical writing style is also religious. That is, Campbell not only describes himself in light of the culture but also in light of his understanding of the divine. All of his autobiographical writings share a religious dimension, but the Campbell they describe has a self-awareness with three dimensions: Campbell the minister, Campbell the reflective ethicist, and Campbell the Southerner.

Conclusion

The decade of the 1960s was a turbulent and formative period for the United States, containing as it did the struggle of African Americans for civil rights and the national debate over the Vietnam War. Opening on an optimistic note with the inauguration of President John F. Kennedy, the decade ended with a large measure of public despair, born of the often violent response to the civil rights movement, the increasing public hesitation about Vietnam, the assassinations of numerous public figures, and the eroding confidence in public authority. When the decade ended, the social disruption created in that period did not. Issues that emerged in the 1960s set the stage for the social, political, and religious environment of the following two decades.

Like the 1960s, Will Campbell was shaped by forces and events that preceded the development of his mature thought. Although his mature thought reached a final clarity with his departure from the National Council of Churches in 1963 and his reaction to the death of Jonathan Daniels in 1965, the preceding years prepared him for these changes. Just as the 1960s colored the social environment of the 1970s and 1980s, so Campbell's departure from the traditional ministry in 1963 shaped his position as a prophetic figure in society. The question remains, however, as to what it means to American and Southern society to have a Will Campbell in its midst. Campbell's prophetic voice is heard in numerous places in society, not the least of which are the Church and the American South.

The events of his sometimes tumultuous life left many indelible impressions on his theology. Perhaps the most prominent was Campbell's suspicion of institutions and his decision to leave the conventional ministry. Campbell did not leave the ministry out of disillusionment with Christianity. Rather, he did so out of his belief that institutional religious organizations and Christian teachings were antithetical. Campbell left the ministry of the institutional church in order to be faithful to Christianity as he understood it. For Campbell, an institution is not a god, and he has refused to give ultimate loyalty to any temporal movement or structure. Yet, Will Campbell is not totally alienated from religious institutions. Like the Hebrew prophets, he stands outside the system while at the same time speaking to the system. A glance at a list of his speaking engagements for any recent year will reveal numerous appearances with different denominational meetings. The institutional church that did so much to shape who Campbell is remains the focus of much of his creative activity.

Campbell is also a prophetic figure for his region, the American South. He was involved in the fight for racial equality very early in the civil rights movement, long before other Southern whites became involved. Few, if any, native southern whites were more involved in the civil rights movement than Campbell. Campbell is a Southerner who embraced his region in all its ironies and ambiguities. He returned to the South to help the region respond to *Brown v. Board of Education* and he has remained there. His relationship with the South is somewhat like his relationship with the institutional church. Campbell affirms his southern identity and applauds the region's embrace of its distinctives. Yet, Campbell knows that the South is not all moonlight and magnolias. As a prophetic figure in the South, he reminds and chastens and corrects those who merely celebrate the best of Southern distinctives without accepting and mourning the worst. Campbell has touched the worlds of religion, social ethics, and Southern culture. His actions, and particularly, his words have made and continue to make a positive contribution to those aspects of the human experience.

Bibliography

PRIMARY SOURCES

Books

Campbell, Will D. *Brother to a Dragonfly*. New York: Seabury, 1977.

_____. *Cecelia's Sin*. Macon: Mercer University Press, 1983.

_____. *The Convention: A Parable*. Atlanta: Peachtree Publishers, 1988.

_____. *Forty Acres and a Goat*. San Francisco: Harper and Row, 1986.

_____. *The Glad River*. Nashville: Rutledge Hill Press, 1982.

_____. *Providence*. Atlanta: Longstreet Press, 1992.

_____. *Race and the Renewal of the Church*. Philadelphia: The Westminster Press, 1962.

_____ and Clayton, Al. *Covenant*. Atlanta: Peachtree Publishers, 1989.

_____ and Holloway, James Y, eds. *". . . and the criminals with him. . ."* New York: Paulist Press, 1973.

_____. *Callings*. New York: Paulist Press, 1974.

_____. *The Failure and the Hope: Essays of Southern Churchmen*. Grand Rapids: William B. Eerdmans, 1972.

_____. *Up to Our Steeples in Politics*. New York: Paulist Press, 1970.

_____ and Hsieh, Jim, illus. *Chester and Chun Ling*. Nashville: Abingdon Press, 1989.

_____, McBride, Will, and Campbell, Bonnie. *God on Earth: The Lord's Prayer for Our Time*. New York: Crossroad, 1983.

Articles

Brett, David [Will D. Campbell]. "Snickness Unto Death: Folk vs. Contemporary Country Music." *Motive*, March 1965, 33-38.

Campbell, Will D. "A Little More Memphis." *New South* 24 (Summer 1969): 28-34.

_____. "About this Issue. . ." *Katallagete*, Winter 1974, 2-3.

_____. "And Now Detroit: What Can We Say Except 'Look Out!'" *Katallagete*, Summer 1967, 1.

_____. "Brer Fox and Brer Tarrypin and the Crisis at Ole Miss." *Christianity and Crisis*, 15 August 1977, 232-236.

_____. "The Church and Riot Control." *Katallagete*, Spring 1968, 2.

_____. "Class of '79." *Katallagete*, Fall 1979, 24-29.

_____. "Clean Up the Botulism." *Southern Exposure*, Summer 1980, 99.

_____. "Commie-Killing: Ethics, Law, Geography." *Christianity and Crisis* 14 May 1984, 174-176.

_____. "The Computer Says 'Repent' (A Fable)." *Faith and Mission* 2 (Fall 1984): 77-81.

_____. "The Day of Our Birth." *Katallagete*, June 1965, 3-5.

_____. "The Death of Willie Gene Carreker." *Race Relations Reporter*, September 1975, 31-37.

_____. "The Display of a Feather." *New South* 17 (January 1962): 7-8.

_____. "The Faith of a Fatalist." *New South* 23 (Spring 1968): 51-57.

_____. "He Ate Yesterday." *The Other Side*, October 1983, 11.

_____. "His Race Was Human Kind." *New South* 25 (Summer 1970): 7-8.

_____. "I Love My Country: Christ Have Mercy." *Motive*, December 1969, 42- 47.

_____. "If We Should Get Serious." *Katallagete*, Winter 1968-1969, 1-2.

_____. "The Inner Life of Church and Synagogue." In *Race: Challenge to Religion*, ed. Mathew Ahman, 9-27. Chicago: Henry Regnery Company, 1963.

_____. "July 19, 1959." *Katallagete*, Fall 1975, 28-32.

_____. "Law and Love in Lowndes." *Katallagete*, June 1965, 11-14.

_____. "A Man Had Two Sons." *Christianity Today*, 10 April 1964, 36-38.

_____. "Movement Hangover: Personal Perspective." *Christianity and Crisis*, 17 March 1986, 77-78.

_____. "Nashville in My Rearview Mirror." *Southern Magazine*, February 1987, 60-64 and 81-82.

_____. "The Negro and the Ballot in the South." *The Interchurch News*, August 1960, 2.

_____. "Nit-Picking a Fine Book." *Christianity and Crisis*, 20 February 1984, 42-43.

_____. "On Getting Sick Together." *Christianity and Crisis*, 1 April 1985, 100-102.

_____. "On Silencing Our Finest." *Christianity and Crisis*, 16 September 1985, 340-342.

_____. "Our Adolescent History." In *Retrospect: 25 Years of School Desegregation (1954-1979)*, eds. Walter J. Leonard, Robert E. Eaker, and Will D. Campbell, 39-48. The School Law Symposium Series. Murfreesboro: Middle Tennessee State University, 1979.

_____. *Oxford Review*, October 1991, 7-8.

_____. "Perhaps; and Maybe." *The Christian Century*, 19 September 1962, 1133.

_____. "Pudor Sit Academia." *Christianity and Crisis*, 25 June 1984, 246-247.

_____. "Quit Picking on Paul." *Christianity and Crisis*, 8 December 1986, 428-430.

_____. "Rednecks and Niggers." *The Progressive*, July 1974, 31.

_____. "Repentance and Politics I: Milestones Into Millstones." *Katallagete* (Winter 1966-1967), 2-4.

_____. "The Role of the Church in the Segregation Crisis." *New South* 17 (June 1962): 3-8.

_____. "The Role of Religion in the Desegregation Controversy." *Union Seminary Quarterly Review* 16 (January 1961): 187-196.

_____. "Rumblings of Rebellion by Southern White Clergy." *Dialogue* 3 (Spring 1964): 124-129.

_____. "The Sit-ins: Passive Resistance or Civil Disobedience?" *Social Action* 27 (January 1961): 14-18.

_____. "Staying Home or Leaving." In *Sense of Place: Mississippi*, eds. Peggy W. Prenshaw and Jessie O. McKee, 14-23. Jackson: University Press of Mississippi, 1979.

_____. "Summit Wishes." *Christianity and Crisis*, 23 December 1985, 508-510.

_____. "Tennessee Disinherits the Wind." *Christianity and Crisis*, 10 July 1967, 165-166.

_____. "The Theological Education of Will Campbell." *Sojourners*, August 1977, 23-26.

_____. "The Time Twelve Women Priests Rewrote the Prayer Book." *Katallagete* (Summer 1976), 42-44.

_____. "Tourist Notes." *Christianity and Crisis*, 16 March 1987, 85-86.

_____. "The Tylenol of Defense." *The Progressive*, December 1982, 66.

_____. "Values and Hazards of Theological Preaching." In *The Pastor as Theologian*, eds. Earl E. Shelp and Ronald H. Sunderland, 67-88. New York: Pilgrim Press, 1988.

_____. "The West Virginia Controversy: Whose Code Do We Follow?" *Christianity and Crisis*, 31 March 1975, 68-73.

_____. "Where There's So Much Smoke." *Sojourners*, December 1979, 19.

_____. "Where to Sit in Scottsboro." *Christianity and Crisis*, 18 July 1977, 189- 191.

_____. "Which is the Real Evil—Snake-Handling or the Establishment Church?" *Southern Voices* (March-April 1974), 41-48.

_____. "White Liberals—All Right in their Place." *Social Progress* (December 1963), 30.

_____. "The World of the Redneck." *Katallagete* (Spring 1974), 34-40.

_____. "Vocation as Grace." *Katallagete* (Fall-Winter 1972), 80-86.

_____ and Holloway, James Y. "An Open Letter to Billy Graham." *Katallagete* (Winter 1971), 1-2.

_____. "Can There Be a Crusade for Christ?" *Katallagete* (Summer 1973), 2-6.

_____. "The End of the World." *Katallagete*, Fall 1970, 2-4.

_____. "The Good News from God in Jesus is Freedom to the Prisoners." *Katallagete* (Winter-Spring 1972), 2-5.

_____. "Our grade is 'F.'" *Katallagete* (Fall 1969), 3-10.

_____. "Truth Language and. . ." *Katallagete* (Summer 1976), 2-4.

_____. "Up to Our Steeples in Politics." *Christianity and Crisis*, 3 February 1969, 36-40.

Ligon, Herschel [Will D. Campbell]. "The Pragmatics of Parity." *Christianity and Crisis*, 6 February 1978, 6-8.

Interviews By Author

Campbell, Will D. First Interview by Author. Phone Call. Waco, Texas to Nashville, Tennessee. 15 May 1992.

_____. Second Interview by Author. Tape Recording. Nashville, Tennessee. 30 December 1992.

_____. Third Interview by Author. Phone Call. Waco, Texas to Nashville, Tennessee. 15 December 1993.

_____. Fourth Interview by Author. Phone Call. Waco, Texas to Nashville, Tennessee. 21 February 1994

Other Interviews

Campbell, Will D. Interview by Robert Dibble. In "An Investigative Study of Faith Development in the Adult Life and Works of Will D. Campbell." Ed.D. diss., N e w O r l e a n s Baptist Theological Seminary, 1984, 145-190.

_____. "Interview with Will Campbell." Interview by Bill McNabb. *The Door*, March/April 1990, 12-15.

_____. "Living Out the Drama: An Interview with Will Campbell." Interview by Kenneth L. Gibble. *The Christian Century*, 30 May 1984, 570-574.

_____. "An Oral History with Will Davis Campbell, Christian Preacher." Interview by Orley B. Caudill. *The Mississippi Oral History Program of the University of Southern Mississippi*, vol. 157. Hattiesburg: University of Southern Mississippi, 1980.

_____. "Prophet, Poet, Preacher-at-Large; A Conversation with Will Campbell." Interview by Norman Bowman. *The Student*, December 1970, 29-31, 39.

Sound Recordings

Campbell, Will D.   Address to the Baptist Public Relations Association. Nashville, Tennessee. 1983. Sound Recording.

_____.   Address to the Ethics Luncheon at The Southern Baptist Theological Seminary. Louisville, Kentucky, 9 March 1983. Sound Recording.

_____. Chapel Address at The Southern Baptist Theological Seminary. Louisville, Kentucky, 9 March 1983. Sound Recording.

_____. Sermon at the Riverside Church. New York, 17 May 1984. Sound Recording.

_____. "What Do We Do About What Has Been Done?" Address to the 51st Annual Ministers Week at Emory University. Atlanta, 1 January 1986. Sound Recording.

SECONDARY SOURCES

Books

Ahlstrom, Sydney. *A Religious History of the American People.* 2 vols. New Haven: Yale University Press, 1972; Image Books, 1975.

Ammerman, Nancy. *Baptist Battles: Social Change and Religious Conflict in the Southern Baptist Convention.* New Brunswick: Rutgers University Press, 1990.

_____, ed. *Southern Baptists Observed: Multiple Perspectives on a Changing Denomination.* Knoxville: The University of Tennessee Press, 1993.

Bailey, Hugh. C. *Liberalism in the New South: Southern Social Reformers and the Progressive Movement.* Coral Gables: University of Miami Press, 1969.

Baldwin, Lewis V. *There is a Balm in Gilead: the Cultural Roots of Martin Luther King, Jr.* Minneapolis: Fortress Press, 1991.

Barnhart, Joe. *The Baptist Holy War.* Austin: The Texas Monthly Press, 1986.

Cabaniss, James A. *A History of the University of Mississippi: Its First Hundred Years.* 2nd ed. Hattiesburg: University College Press of Mississippi, 1971.

Carter, Dan. *The Scottsboro Boys: A Tragedy of the American South.* Baton Rouge: Louisiana State University Press, 1969.

Chalmers, David Mark. *Hooded Americanism: the History of the Ku Klux Klan.* New York: New Viewpoints, 1981.

Connelly, Thomas L. *Will Campbell and the Soul of the South.* New York: Continuum, 1982.

Daniels, Jonathan Myrick. *The Jon Daniels Story, with his Letters and Papers.* Edited by William J. Schneider. New York: Seabury Press, 1967.

Dunbar, Anthony. *Against the Grain: Southern Radicals and Prophets, 1929-1959.* Charlottesville: University Press of Virginia, 1981.

Eagles, Charles W. *Outside Agitator: Jon Daniels and the Civil Rights Movement in Alabama.* Chapel Hill: The University of North Carolina Press, 1993.

Eakin, Paul John, ed. *American Autobiography: Retrospect and Prospect.* Madison: University of Wisconsin Press, 1991.

East, P. D. *The Magnolia Jungle: The Life, Times, and Education of a Southern Editor.* New York: Simon and Schuster, 1960.

Egerton, John. *A Mind to Stay Here: Profiles from the South.* New York: Macmillan, 1970.

Eighmy, John Lee. *Churches in Cultural Captivity: A History of the Social Attitudes of Southern Baptists.* rev. ed. With an introduction, conclusion, and bibliography by Samuel S. Hill. Knoxville: The University of Tennessee Press, 1987.

Eller, Vernard. *Christian Anarchy.* Grand Rapids: Eerdmans, 1987.

Ellul, Jacques. *Anarchy and Christianity.* 1st Eng. ed. Translated by Geoffrey Bromiley. Grand Rapids: Eerdmans, 1991.

Fast, Howard. *Freedom Road.* New York: Duell, Sloan, and Pearce, 1944.

Findlay, James. *Church People in the Struggle: The National Council of Churches and the Black Freedom Movement, 1950-1970.* Religion in America Series. New York: Oxford University Press, 1993.

Frady, Marshall. *Billy Graham: A Parable of American Righteousness.* Boston: Little, Brown, 1979.

_____. *Southerners: A Journalist's Odyssey.* New York: New American Library, 1980.

Gaillard, Frye. *Race, Rock, and Religion: Profiles from a Southern Journalist.* New York: East Woods Press, 1982.

Garrow, David J. *Bearing the Cross: Martin Luther King, Jr. and the Southern Christian Leadership Conference.* 1st ed. New York: Morrow, 1986.

Goldberg, Kenneth L. *Theology and Narrative: A Critical Introduction.* Nashville: Abingdon, 1981.

Goldfield, David R. *Black, White, and Southern: Race Relations and Southern Culture, 1940 to the Present.* Baton Rouge: Louisiana State University Press, 1990.

Hill, Samuel S., Jr., ed. *On Jordan's Stormy Banks: Religion in the South: A Southern Exposure Profile*. Macon, Georgia: Mercer University Press, 1983.

_____. *The South and the North in American Religion*. Athens, Georgia: University of Georgia Press, 1980.

_____. *Southern Churches in Crisis*. 1st ed. New York: Holt, Rinehart, and Winston, 1967.

Hilton, Bruce. *The Delta Ministry*. New York: Macmillan, 1969.

Hoffmeyer, Oscar. *Louisiana College 75 Years: A Pictorial History*. Pineville, Louisiana: Louisiana College, 1981.

Holman, C. Hugh. *The Immoderate Past: The Southern Writer and History*. Athens: University of Georgia Press, 1977.

Kaplan, Kaplan, et al. *A Bibliography of American Autobiographies*. Madison: University of Wisconsin Press, 1962.

Kluger, Richard. *Simple Justice: the History of Brown v. Board of Education and Black America's Struggle for Equality*. 1st ed. New York: Knopf, 1976.

Leonard, Bill. *God's Last and Only Hope*. Grand Rapids: Eerdmans Publishing Company, 1990.

Littell, Franklin. *The Anabaptist View of the Church*. 2nd rev. ed. Boston: Starr King Press, 1958.

Louisiana Baptist Convention. *Annual of the Louisiana Baptist Convention*. Baton Rouge: Louisiana State Convention, 1953.

Lumpkin, William L., ed. *Baptist Confessions of Faith*. Philadelphia: Judson Press, 1959.

McAdam, Doug. *Freedom Summer*. New York: Oxford University Press, 1988.

McClendon, James William, Jr. *Biography as Theology*. Nashville: Abingdon Press, 1974.

McLoughlin, William Gerald. *Revivals, Awakenings, and Reform: an Essay on Religion and Social Change in America, 1607-1977*. Chicago: University of Chicago Press, 1978.

Menno Simons. *The Complete Writings of Menno Simons*. corrected ed., trans. Leonard Verduin and ed. J. C. Wenger, with a biography by Harold S. Bender. Scottdale, Pennsylvania: Herald Press, 1956.

Moore, R. Laurence. *Religious Outsiders and the Making of Americans*. New York: Oxford University Press, 1986.

Morris, Aldon. *The Origins of the Civil Rights Movement: Black Communities Organizing for Change*. New York: Free Press, 1984.

Myrdal, Gunnar. *An American Dilemma: The Negro Problem and Modern Democracy*. New York: Harper and Row, 1962.

Olney, James, ed. *Autobiography: Essays Theoretical and Critical*. Princeton: Princeton University Press, 1980.

_____. *Metaphors of Self: The Meaning of Autobiography*. Princeton: Princeton University Press, 1972.

_____. *Studies in Autobiography*. New York: Oxford University Press, 1988.

Pope, Liston. *Millhands and Preachers, a Study of Gastonia*. Yale Studies in Religious Education, 15. New Haven: Yale University Press, 1942.

Queen, Edward L. *In the South the Baptists are the Center of Gravity: Southern Baptists and Social Change, 1930-1980*. Brooklyn: Carlson, 1991.

Reed, John Shelton. *The Enduring South: Subcultural Persistence in Mass Society*. Lexington, Massachusetts: Lexington Books, 1972.

_____. *One South: an Ethnic Approach to Regional Culture*. Baton Rouge: Louisiana State University Press, 1982.

Rosenberg, Ellen MacGilvra. *The Southern Baptists: A Subculture in Transition*. Knoxville: The University of Tennessee Press, 1989.

Rouse, Ruth, and Neill, Stephen Charles, eds. 2nd ed. 2 vols. *A History of the Ecumenical Movement*. Philadelphia: Westminster Press, 1967.

Sayre, Robert F. *The Examined Self: Benjamin Franklin, Henry Adams, Henry James*. Madison: University of Wisconsin Press, 1988.

Schneider, William J. *American Martyr: The Jon Daniels Story*. Milwaukee: Morehouse Publishing, 1992.

Skates, John Ray. *Mississippi: A Bicentennial History*. New York: W. W. Norton and Company, 1979.

Silver, James W. *Mississippi: The Closed Society*. new ed. New York: Harcourt, Brace, and World, 1966.

————. *Running Scared: Silver in Mississippi*. Jackson: University Press of Mississippi, 1984.

Stone, Albert E., ed. *The American Autobiography: A Collection of Critical Essays*. Englewood: New Jersey, 1981.

Straub, Deborah A., ed. "Campbell, Will D(avis), 1924-." *Contemporary Authors: New Revision Series*, vol. 22. Detroit: Gail Research, 1988.

United States Commission on Civil Rights. *School Desegregation in Little Rock, Arkansas: A Staff Report on the United States Commission on Civil Rights*. Washington: United States Commission on Civil Rights, 1977.

Whitfield Stephen J. *A Death in the Delta: The Story of Emmett Till*. New York: The Free Press, 1988.

Williams, George H. *The Radical Reformation*. Philadelphia: Westminster Press, 1962.

Williamson, Joel. *A Rage for Order: Black/White Relations in the American South Since Emancipation*. New York: Oxford University Press, 1986.

Wilson, Charles Reagan. "God's Project: The Southern Civil Religion, 1920-1980." In *Religion and the Life of the Nation: American Recoveries*, ed. Rowland Sherrill. Urbana: University Of Illinois Press, 1990.

Woodward, C. Vann. *The Burden of Southern History*. rev. ed. Baton Rouge: Louisiana State University Press, 1968.

Wright, Lawrence. *Saints and Sinners*. New York: Alfred A. Knopf, 1993.

Journal Articles

Bainton, Roland. "The Left Wing of the Reformation." *Journal of Religion* 21 (1941): 125-134.

Bergland, Betty. "Autobiography and American Culture." *American Quarterly* 45 (September 1993): 445-458.

Findlay, James. "Religion and Politics in the Sixties: The Churches and the Civil Rights Act of 1964." *The Journal of American History* 80 (June 1990): 67-92.

Martin, Robert. "A Prophet's Pilgrimage: The Religious Radicalism of Howard Anderson Kester, 1921-1941." *Journal of Southern History* 48 (1982): 511-530.

_____. "Critique of Southern Society and Vision of a New Order: The Fellowship of Southern Churchmen, 1934-1957." *Church History* 52 (1983): 66-80.

Periodicals and Newspapers

Boers, Arthur. "Will Campbell: In the Great Company of God's Grace." *The Other Side*, September 1987, 40-44.

Bracker, Milton. "Mississippi Parley on Religion Periled by Ban on Minister." *New York Times*, 11 February 1956, 1 and 38.

_____. "Mississippi Plans a Religious Week." *New York Times*, 12 February 1956, 86.

Demaret, Kent. "Spirit." *People*, 17 July 1978, 39 and 42.

Egerton, John. "About Will Campbell." *New South* 22 (Fall 1967): 66-76.

Ellul, Jacques. "Anarchism and Christianity." *Katallagete*, Fall 1980, 14-24.

Frady, Marshall. "Fighter for Forgotten Men." *Life*, 16 June 1972, 57-66.

Gaillard, Frye. "Preacher to the Damned." *The Progressive*, December 1982, 40-44.

"Good Will." *Newsweek*, 8 May 1972, 84.

Hargus, Relma. "Colorful Baptist 'Non-Pastor' Writes Book About Convention." *SBC Today*, August 1988, 15.

The Petal Paper. First Search, 4178093.

Pleasants, Phyllis R. "Seeker After Freedom." *Baptist Peacemaker*, January 1989, 1 and 3-4.

Sandon, Leo Jr. "From Social Gospel to Anabaptism." *The Bulletin of the Center for the Study of Southern Religion and Culture* 1 (Summer 1977): 2-7.

Sherrill, Robert. "Power in Their Blood: Four Evangelists and the Varieties of Religious Experience Down South." *Esquire*, June 1968, 731-755.

Encylopedias

Bender, Harold S., ed. *The Mennonite Encyclopedia: A Comprehensive Reference Work on the Anabaptist-Mennonite Movement.* Hillsboro, Kansas: Mennonite Brethren Publishing House, 1955-1959.

Hill, Samuel S., Jr., ed. *The Encyclopedia of Religion in the South.* Macon, Georgia: Mercer University Press, 1984.

Lippy, Charles H., and Williams, Peter W., eds. *Encyclopedia of the American Religious Experience: Studies of Traditions and Movements.* New York: Charles Scribner's Sons, 1988.

Reid, Daniel, et al., eds. *Dictionary of Christianity in America.* Downers Grove, Illinois: Intervarsity Press, 1990.

Wilson, Charles Reagan, and Ferris, William, eds. *Encyclopedia of Southern Culture.* Chapel Hill: University of North Carolina Press, 1989.

Reviews

Anker, Roy M. "A Handhold on Faith." Review of *The Glad River*, by Will D. Campbell. In *The Reformed Journal* 33 (March 1983): 20.

Caldwell, Wayne T. "Reviewer Claims 'The Convention' Readably Reveals SBC Conflicts." Review of *The Convention: A Parable*, by Will D. Campbell. In *SBC Today*, March 1989, 18.

Clancy, Thomas H. "Points of the Compass, of the Cortex, of the Cosmos." Review of *Brother to a Dragonfly*, by Will D. Campbell. In *America*, 3 June 1978, 450.

_____. Review of *Up to Our Steeples in Politics*, by Will D. Campbell and James Y. Holloway. In *America*, 1 January 1971, 53-54.

Cooper, Robert M. Review of *Brother to a Dragonfly*, by Will D. Campbell. In *Anglican Theological Review* 61 (October 1979): 529.

Egerton, John. "Love and Blood." Review of *Brother to a Dragonfly*, by Will D. Campbell. In *The Progressive*, February 1978, 42-43.

Eichelberger, William L. Review of *The Failure and the Hope: Essays of Southern Churchmen*, by Will D. Campbell and James Y. Holloway, eds. In *Review and Expositor* 70 (Fall 1973): 535-537.

Hauerwas, Stanley. "Autobiography and Politics." Review of *Brother to a Dragonfly*, by Will D. Campbell and *Once to Every Man*, by William Sloane Coffin, Jr. In *Worldview* 21 (April 1977): 49-51.

Hauser, Gordon. "Search for a Real Baptist." Review of *The Glad River*, by Will D. Campbell. In *Sojourners*, January 1982, 38-39.

Kennedy, Thomas D. "Pastor Will." Review of *Forty Acres and a Goat*, by Will D. Campbell. In *The Reformed Journal* 37 (May 1987): 28-29.

King, Larry L. "Love Among the Red-necks." Review of *Brother to a Dragonfly*, by Will D. Campbell. In *Saturday Review*, 12 December 1977, 44-46.

Lederer, Norman. "Southern Anguish." Review of *The Failure and the Hope: Essays of Southern Churchmen*, by Will D. Campbell and James Y. Holloway, eds. In *The Christian Century*, 4 April 1973, 400.

Marty, Myron A. Review of *Forty Acres and a Goat*, by Will D. Campbell. In *The Christian Century*, 28 January 1987, 89-90.

McSwain, Larry L. Review of *Brother to a Dragonfly*, by Will D. Campbell. In *Perspectives in Religious Studies* 5 (Fall 1978): 217-218.

Narké. "Dragonflies." Review of *Brother to a Dragonfly*, by Will D. Campbell. *Katallagete*, Spring 1978, 40-42.

Ponstein, Lambert J. Review of *The Failure and the Hope: Essays of Southern Churchmen*, by Will D. Campbell and James Y. Holloway, eds. In *The Reformed Review* 27 (Fall 1973): 34-35.

Rossiter, M. Larkin. Review of *Brother to a Dragonfly*, by Will D. Campbell. In *Union Seminary Quarterly Review* 33(Winter 1978): 105-106.

Stringfellow, William, et. al. "The Steeples in Perspective: Four Views." Review of *Up to Our Steeples in Politics*, Will D. Campbell and James Y. Holloway. In *Christianity and Crisis*, 3 March 1969, 40-44.

Taylor, John. "I'm Way Down in Dixie, but I Feel Like I Ain't Nowhere." Review of *Brother to a Dragonfly*, by Will D. Campbell, *Witness in Philadelphia*, by Florence Mars, and *In Search of the Silent South*, by Morton Sosna. In *The Nation*, 3 December 1977, 597-598.

Vance, Melvin. Review of *Up to Our Steeples in Politics*, by Will D. Campbell and James Y. Holloway. In *Union Seminary Quarterly Review* 28 (Winter 1973): 177-181.

Yardley, Jonathan. "A Calling to Help." Review of *Brother to a Dragonfly*, by Will D. Campbell. In *New York Times Book Review*, 27 November 1977, 10 and 52.

_____. "Will Campbell's Novel of Love, Death, and Redemption." Review of *The Glad River*, by Will D. Campbell. *Book World*, 11 April 1982, 3.

Unpublished Works

Dibble, Robert. "An Investigative Study of Faith Development in the Adult Life and Works of Will D. Campbell." Ed.D. diss., New Orleans Baptist Theological Seminary, 1984.

Jimmerson, Robin. "A Sociological Analysis of the Prophetic Ministry of Will D. Campbell." Ph.D. diss., Southern Baptist Theological Seminary, 1990.

Kirkley, Evelyn A. "The Turning of Dreams into Deeds: Clarence Jordan and Will Campbell." B.A. honors thesis, College of William and Mary, 1982.

Shoemaker, H. Stephen. "Eschaton and Apocalypse in Contemporary Christian Ethics: A Study of the Ethics of Jacques Ellul and Will Campbell and James Holloway." M.Div. thesis, Union Theological Seminary, 1974.

Weaver-Williams, Lynda. "Walker Percy and Will Campbell: A Theological-Ethical Analysis." Ph.D. diss., Southern Baptist Theological Seminary, 1981.

Index